SOCIALISM

UTOPIAN AND SCIENTIFIC

BY

FREDERICK ENGELS

TRANSLATED BY EDWARD AVELING
D.Sc., Fellow of University College, London

WITH A SPECIAL INTRODUCTION BY THE AUTHOR

CHICAGO:
CHARLES H. KERR & COMPANY
1907

Note by the American Publisher

This little volume is an exact reproduction of the standard English translation of one of the most noteworthy books of the nineteenth century. To Engels scarcely less than to Marx is due the impetus to clear thinking which has placed the Socialism of continental Europe in a commanding position, where it is recognized as the hope of the workers and the terror of the rulers. SOCIALISM UTOPIAN AND SCIENTIFIC has been translated into the language of every capitalist nation, and wherever it has gone it has been an inspiration.

In America it has thus far been known by the rather expensive edition (imported by Charles Scribner's Sons) from which this edition is reprinted, and by an earlier and somewhat inferior translation, printed in fine type and published without the remarkable introduction written by Engels in 1892 and here presented.

The appendix on the origin of the German Mark has been omitted from the present edition for the reason that the development of agriculture in this country has been so different from that in Europe that this appendix would be more confusing than helpful to the average American reader.

Signs are not wanting that the growth of Socialism in America will be rapid. The easy victory of organized capital represented in the Republican party, over the discordant elements of the now superfluous middle class, leaves a clear field for the organization of hand workers and brain workers into the party destined to build a new and better social order out of the crumbling ruins of capitalism.

CHARLES H. KERR.

February, 1900.

INTRODUCTION.

THE present little book is, originally, a part of a larger whole. About 1875, Dr. E. Dühring, *privat-docent* at Berlin University, suddenly and rather clamorously announced his conversion to Socialism, and presented the German public not only with an elaborate Socialist theory, but also with a complete practical plan for the reorganisation of society. As a matter of course, he fell foul of his predecessors; above all, he honoured Marx by pouring out upon him the full vials of his wrath.

This took place about the time when the two sections of the Socialist party in Germany—Eisenachers and Lassallians—had just effected their fusion, and thus obtained not only an immense increase of strength, but, what was more, the faculty of employing the whole of this strength against the common enemy. The Socialist party in Germany was fast becoming a power. But to make it a power, the first condition was that the newly-conquered unity should not be imperilled. And Dr. Dühring openly proceeded to form around himself a sect, the nucleus of a future separate party. It thus became necessary to take up the gauntlet thrown down to us, and to fight out the struggle whether we liked it or not.

This, however, though it might not be an over difficult, was evidently a long-winded, business. As is well known, we Germans are of a terribly ponderous *Gründlichkeit*, radical profundity or profound radicality, whatever you may like to call it. Whenever anyone of us expounds what he considers a new doctrine, he has first to elaborate it into an all-comprising system. He has to prove that both the first principles of logic and the fundamental laws of the universe had existed from all eternity for no other purpose than to ultimately lead to this newly-discovered, crowning theory. And Dr. Dühring, in this respect, was quite up to the national mark. Nothing less than a complete " System of Philosophy," mental, moral, natural, and historical ; a complete " System of Political Economy and Socialism ;" and, finally, a " Critical History of Political Economy "—three big volumes in octavo, heavy extrinsically and intrinsically, three army-corps of arguments mobilised against all previous philosophers and economists in general, and against Marx in particular—in fact, an attempt at a complete " revolution in science "—these were what I should have to tackle. I had to treat of all and every possible subject, from the concepts of time and space to Bimetallism ; from the eternity of matter and motion to the perishable nature of moral ideas ; from Darwin's natural selection to the education of youth in a future society. Anyhow, the systematic comprehensiveness of my opponent gave me the opportunity of developing, in opposition to him, and in a more connected form than had pre-

viously been done, the views held by Marx and myself
on this great variety of subjects. And that was the
principal reason which made me undertake this otherwise ungrateful task.

My reply was first published in a series of articles
in the Leipzig "Vorwärts," the chief organ of the
Socialist party, and later on as a book: "Herrn
Eugen Dühring's Umwälzung der Wissenschaft" (Mr.
E. Dühring's "Revolution in Science"), a second
edition of which appeared in Zürich, 1886.

At the request of my friend, Paul Lafargue, now
representative of Lille in the French Chamber of
Deputies, I arranged three chapters of this book as a
pamphlet, which he translated and published in 1880,
under the title: "*Socialisme utopique et Socialisme
scientifique.*" From this French text a Polish and a
Spanish edition were prepared. In 1883, our German
friends brought out the pamphlet in the original
language. Italian, Russian, Danish, Dutch, and
Roumanian translations, based upon the German
text, have since been published. Thus, with the
present English edition, this little book circulates in
ten languages. I am not aware that any other
Socialist work, not even our "Communist Manifesto"
of 1848 or Marx's "Capital," has been so often
translated. In Germany it has had four editions of
about 20,000 copies in all.

The Appendix, "the Mark," was written with the
intention of spreading among the German Socialist
party some elementary knowledge of the history and
development of landed property in Germany. This

seemed all the more necessary at a time when the
assimilation by that party of the working-people of
the towns was in a fair way of completion, and when
the agricultural labourers and peasants had to be
taken in hand. This appendix has been included in
the translation, as the original forms of tenure of land
common to all Teutonic tribes, and the history of
their decay, are even less known in England than in
Germany. I have left the text as it stands in the
original, without alluding to the hypothesis recently
started by Maxim Kovalevsky, according to which
the partition of the arable and meadow lands among
the members of the Mark was preceded by their
being cultivated for joint-account by a large patriarchal family community embracing several genera-
tions (as exemplified by the still existing South
Slavonian Zadruga); and that the partition, later on,
took place when the community had increased, so as
to become too unwieldy for joint-account management. Kovalevsky is probably quite right, but the
matter is still *sub judice.*

The economic terms used in this work, as far as
they are new, agree with those used in the English
edition of Marx's "Capital." We call "production of
commodities" that economic phase where articles are
produced not only for the use of the producers, but also
for purposes of exchange; that is, *as commodities*, not
as use-values. This phase extends from the first
beginnings of production for exchange down to our
present time; it attains its full development under
capitalist production only, that is, under conditions

where the capitalist, the owner of the means of production, employs, for wages, labourers, people deprived of all means of production except their own labour-power, and pockets the excess of the selling price of the products over his outlay. We divide the history of industrial production since the Middle Ages into three periods: (1) handicraft, small master craftsmen with a few journeymen and apprentices, where each labourer produces the complete article; (2) manufacture, where greater numbers of workmen, grouped in one large establishment, produce the complete article on the principle of division of labour, each workman performing only one partial operation, so that the product is complete only after having passed successively through the hands of all; (3) modern industry, where the product is produced by machinery driven by power, and where the work of the labourer is limited to superintending and correcting the performances of the mechanical agent.

I am perfectly aware that the contents of this work will meet with objection from a considerable portion of the British public. But if we Continentals had taken the slightest notice of the prejudices of British "respectability," we should be even worse off than we are. This book defends what we call "historical materialism," and the word materialism grates upon the ears of the immense majority of British readers. "Agnosticism" might be tolerated, but materialism is utterly inadmissible.

And yet the original home of all modern materialism, from the seventeenth century onwards, is England;

"Materialism is the natural-born son of Great Britain. Already the British schoolman, Duns Scotus, asked, 'whether it was impossible for matter o think?'

"In order to effect this miracle, he took refuge in God's omnipotence, *i.e.,* he made theology preach materialism. Moreover, he was a nominalist. Nominalism, the first form of materialism, is chiefly found among the English schoolmen.

"The real progenitor of · English materialism is Bacon. To him natural philosophy is the only true philosophy, and physics based upon the experience of the senses is the chiefest part of natural philosophy. Anaxagoras and his homoiomeriæ, Democritus and his atoms, he often quotes as his authorities. According to him the senses are infallible and the source of all knowledge. All science is based on experience, and consists in subjecting the data furnished by the senses to a rational method of investigation. Induction, analysis, comparison, observation, experiment, are the principal forms of such a rational method. Among the qualities inherent in matter, motion is the first and foremost, not only in the form of mechanical and mathematical motion, but chiefly in the form of an impulse, a vital spirit, a tension — or a 'qual,' to use a term of Jacob Böhme's [1]—of matter.

[1] "Qual" is a philosophical play upon words. Qual literally means torture, a pain which drives to action of some kind ; at the same time the mystic Böhme puts into the German word something of the meaning of the Latin *qualitas;* his "qual"

"In Bacon, its first creator, materialism still occludes within itself the germs of a many-sided development. On the one hand, matter, surrounded by a sensuous, poetic glamour, seems to attract man's whole entity by winning smiles. On the other, the aphoristically formulated doctrine pullulates with inconsistencies imported from theology.

"In its further evolution, materialism becomes one-sided. Hobbes is the man who systematises Baconian materialism. Knowledge based upon the senses loses its poetic blossom, it passes into the abstract experience of the mathematician; geometry is proclaimed as the queen of sciences. Materialism takes to misanthropy. If it is to overcome its opponent, misanthropic, fleshless spiritualism, and that on the latter's own ground, materialism has to chastise its own flesh and turn ascetic. Thus, from a sensual, it passes into an intellectual, entity; but thus, too, it evolves all the consistency, regardless of consequences, characteristic of the intellect.

"Hobbes, as Bacon's continuator, argues thus: if all human knowledge is furnished by the senses, then our concepts and ideas are but the phantoms, divested of their sensual forms, of the real world. Philosophy can but give names to these phantoms. One name may be applied to more than one of them. There may even be names of names. It would imply a contradiction if, on the one hand, we maintained that

was the activating principle arising from, and promoting in its turn, the spontaneous development of the thing, relation, or person subject to it, in contradistinction to a pain inflicted from without.

all ideas had their origin in the world of sensation,
and, on the other, that a word was more than a word;
that besides the beings known to us by our senses,
beings which are one and all individuals, there existed
also beings of a general, not individual, nature. An
unbodily substance is the same absurdity as an
unbodily body. Body, being, substance, are but
different terms for the same reality. *It is impossible
to separate thought from matter that thinks.* This
matter is the substratum of all changes going on in
the world. The word infinite is meaningless, unless
it states that our mind is capable of performing an
endless process of addition. Only material things
being perceptible to us, we cannot know anything
about the existence of God. My own existence alone
is certain. Every human passion is a mechanical
movement which has a beginning and an end. The
objects of impulse are what we call good. Man is
subject to the same laws as nature. Power and
freedom are identical.

"Hobbes had systematised Bacon, without, however, furnishing a proof for Bacon's fundamental
principle, the origin of all human knowledge from
the world of sensation. It was Locke who, in his
Essay on the Human Understanding, supplied this
proof.

"Hobbes had shattered the theistic prejudices of
Baconian materialism; Collins, Dodwall, Coward,
Hartley, Priestley similarly shattered the last
theological bars that still hemmed-in Locke's sen-
sationalism. At all events, for practical material-

ists, Theism is but an easy-going way of getting rid of religion."[1]

Thus Karl Marx wrote about the British origin of modern materialism. If Englishmen nowadays do not exactly relish the compliment he paid their ancestors, more's the pity. It is none the less undeniable that Bacon, Hobbes, and Locke are the fathers of that brilliant school of French materialists which made the eighteenth century, in spite of all battles on land and sea won over Frenchmen by Germans and Englishmen, a pre-eminently French century, even before that crowning French Revolution, the results of which we outsiders, in England as well as in Germany, are still trying to acclimatise.

There is no denying it. About the middle of this century, what struck every cultivated foreigner who set up his residence in England, was, what he was then bound to consider the religious bigotry and stupidity of the English respectable middle-class. We, at that time, were all materialists, or, at least, very advanced freethinkers, and to us it appeared inconceivable that almost all educated people in England should believe in all sorts of impossible miracles, and that even geologists like Buckland and Mantell should contort the facts of their science so as not to clash too much with the myths of the book of Genesis; while, in order to find people who dared to use their own intellectual faculties with regard to religious matters, you had to go amongst the uneducated, the

[1] Marx and Engels, "Die Heilige Familie," Frankfurt a. M. 1845, pp. 201-204.

"great unwashed," as they were then called, the working people, especially the Owenite Socialists.

But England has been "civilised" since then. The
exhibition of 1851 sounded the knell of English
insular exclusiveness. England became gradually
internationalised, in diet, in manners, in ideas; so
much so that I begin to wish that some English
manners and customs had made as much headway on
the Continent as other continental habits have made
here. Anyhow, the introduction and spread of salad-
oil (before 1851 known only to the aristocracy) has
been accompanied by a fatal spread of continental
scepticism in matters religious, and it has come to
this, that agnosticism, though not yet considered
"the thing" quite as much as the Church of England,
is yet very nearly on a par, as far as respectability
goes, with Baptism, and decidedly ranks above the
Salvation Army. And I cannot help believing that
under these circumstances it will be consoling to
many who sincerely regret and condemn this progress
of infidelity, to learn that these "new-fangled notions"
are not of foreign origin, are not "made in Germany,"
like so many other articles of daily use, but are undoubtedly Old English, and that their British origina-
tors two hundred years ago went a good deal further
than their descendants now dare to venture.

What, indeed, is agnosticism, but, to use an ex-
pressive Lancashire term, "shamefaced" materialism?
The agnostic's conception of Nature is materialistic
throughout. The entire natural world is governed
by law, and absolutely excludes the intervention of

action from without. But, he adds, we have no means either of ascertaining or of disproving the existence of some Supreme Being beyond the known universe. Now, this might hold good at the time when Laplace, to Napoleon's question, why in the great astronomer's *Mécanique céleste* the Creator was not even mentioned, proudly replied : *Je n'avais pas besoin de cette hypothese.* But nowadays, in our evolutionary conception of the universe, there is absolutely no room for either a Creator or a Ruler ; and to talk of a Supreme Being shut out from the whole existing world, implies a contradiction in terms, and, as it seems to me, a gratuitous insult to the feelings of religious people.

Again, our agnostic admits that all our knowledge is based upon the information imparted to us by our senses. But, he adds, how do we know that our senses give us correct representations of the objects we perceive through them ? And he proceeds to inform us that, whenever he speaks of objects or their qualities, he does in reality not mean these objects and qualities, of which he cannot know anything for certain, but merely the impressions which they have produced on his senses. Now, this line of reasoning seems undoubtedly hard to beat by mere argumentation. But before there was argumentation, there was action. *Im Anfang war die That.* And human action had solved the difficulty long before human ingenuity invented it. The proof of the pudding is in the eating. From the moment we turn to our own use these objects, according to the qualities we per-

ceive in them, we put to an infallible test the correct-
ness or otherwise of our sense-perceptions. If
these perceptions have been wrong, then our estimate
of the use to which an object can be turned must
also be wrong, and our attempt must fail. But if we
succeed in accomplishing our aim, if we find that the
object does agree with our idea of it, and does answer
the purpose we intended it for, then that is positive
proof that our perceptions of it and of its qualities, *so
far*, agree with reality outside ourselves. And whenever we find ourselves face to face with a failure, then
we generally are not long in making out the cause
that made us fail ; we find that the perception upon
which we acted was either incomplete and superficial,
or combined with the results of other perceptions in a
way not warranted by them—what we call defective
reasoning. So long as we take care to train and to
use our senses properly, and to keep our action within
the limits prescribed by perceptions properly made
and properly used, so long we shall find that the
result of our action proves the conformity of our perceptions with the objective nature of the things
perceived. Not in one single instance, so far, have
we been led to the conclusion that our sense-perceptions, scientifically controlled, induce in our minds
ideas respecting the outer world that are, by their
very nature, at variance with reality, or that there is
an inherent incompatibility between the outer world
and our sense-perceptions of it.

But then come the Neo-Kantian agnostics and say :
We may correctly perceive the qualities of a thing,

but we cannot by any sensible or mental process grasp the thing in itself. This "thing in itself" is beyond our ken. To this Hegel, long since, has replied · If you know all the qualities of a thing, you know the thing itself; nothing remains but the fact that the said thing exists without us; and when your senses have taught you that fact, you have grasped the last remnant of the thing in itself, Kant's celebrated unknowable *Ding an sich.* To which it may be added, that in Kant's time our knowledge of natural objects was indeed so fragmentary that he might well suspect, behind the little we knew about each of them, a mysterious "thing in itself." But one after another these ungraspable things have been grasped, analysed, and, what is more, *reproduced* by the giant progress of science ; and what we can produce, we certainly cannot consider as unknowable. To the chemistry of the first half of this century organic substances were such mysterious objects; now, we learn to build them up one after another from their chemical elements without the aid of organic processes. Modern chemists declare that as soon as the chemical constitution of no matter what body is known, it can be built up from its elements. We are still far from knowing the constitution of the highest organic substances, the albuminous bodies ; but there is no reason why we should not, if only after centuries, arrive at that knowledge and, armed with it, produce artificial albumen. But if we arrive at that, we shall at the same time have produced organic life, for life, from its lowest to its highest forms, is but the normal mode of existence of albuminous bodies.

As soon, however, as our agnostic has made these formal mental reservations, he talks and acts as the rank materialist he at bottom is. He may say that, as far as we know, matter and motion, or as it is now called, energy, can neither be created nor destroyed, but that we have no proof of their not having been created at some time or other. But if you try to use this admission against him in any particular case, he will quickly put you out of court. If he admits the possibility of spiritualism *in abstracto*, he will have none of it *in concreto*. As far as we know and can know, he will tell you there is no Creator and no Ruler of the universe; as far as we are concerned, matter and energy can neither be created nor annihilated; for us, mind is a mode of energy, a function of the brain; all we know is that the material world is governed by immutable laws, and so forth. Thus, as far as he is a scientific man, as far as he *knows* anything, he is a materialist; outside his science, in spheres about which he knows nothing, he translates his ignorance into Greek and calls it agnosticism.

At all events, one thing seems clear: even if I was an agnostic, it is evident that I could not describe the conception of history sketched out in this little book, as "historical agnosticism." Religious people would laugh at me, agnostics would indignantly ask, was I going to make fun of them? And thus I hope even British respectability will not be overshocked if I use, in English as well as in so many other languages, the term, "historical materialism," to designate that

view of the course of history, which seeks the ultimate
cause and the great moving power of all important
historic events in the economic development of society,
in the changes in the modes of production and exchange, in the consequent division of society into dis-
tinct classes, and in the struggles of these classes
against one another.

This indulgence will perhaps be accorded to me all
the sooner if I show that historical materialism may
be of advantage even to British respectability. I have
mentioned the fact, that about forty or fifty years ago,
any cultivated foreigner settling in England was
struck by what he was then bound to consider the
religious bigotry and stupidity of the English respect
able middle-class. I am now going to prove that the
respectable English middle-class of that time was not
quite as stupid as it looked to the intelligent foreigner.
Its religious leanings can be explained.

When Europe emerged from the Middle Ages, the
rising middle-class of the towns constituted its revolutionary element. It had conquered a recognised
position within mediæval feudal organisation, but this
position, also, had become too narrow for its expansive
power. The development of the middle-class, the
bourgeoisie, became incompatible with the maintenance of the feudal system; the feudal system, therefore, had to fall.

But the great international centre of feudalism was
the Roman Catholic Church. It united the whole of
feudalised Western Europe, in spite of all internal
wars, into one grand political system, opposed as much

to the schismatic Greeks as to the Mohammedan
countries. It surrounded feudal institutions with the
halo of divine consecration. It had organised its own
hierarchy on the feudal model, and, lastly, it was itself
by far the most powerful feudal lord, holding, as it
did, fully one-third of the soil of the Catholic world.
Before profane feudalism could be successfully attacked
in each country and in detail, this, its sacred central
organisation, had to be destroyed

Moreover, parallel with the rise of the middle-class
went on the great revival of science, astronomy,
mechanics, physics, anatomy physiology, were again
cultivated And the bourgeoisie, for the development
of its industrial production, required a science which
ascertained the physical properties of natural objects
and the modes of action of the forces of Nature. Now
up to then science had but been the humble handmaid
of the Church, had not been allowed to overstep the
limits set by faith, and for that reason had been no
science at all. Science rebelled against the Church;
the bourgeoisie could not do without science, and,
therefore, had to join in the rebellion.

The above, though touching but two of the points
where the rising middle-class was bound to come into
collision with the established religion, will be sufficient
to show, first, that the class most directly interested
in the struggle against the pretensions of the Roman
Church was the bourgeoisie; and second, that every
struggle against feudalism, at that time, had to take
on a religious disguise, had to be directed against the
Church in the first instance. But if the universities

and the traders of the cities started the cry, it was sure to find, and did find, a strong echo in the masses of the country people, the peasants, who everywhere had to struggle for their very existence with their feudal lords, spiritual and temporal.

The long fight of the bourgeoisie against feudalism culminated in three great, decisive battles.

The first was what is called the Protestant Reformation in Germany   The war-cry raised against the Church by Luther was responded to by two insurrections of a political nature: first, that of the lower nobility under Franz von Sickingen (1523), then the great Peasants' War, 1525. Both were defeated, chiefly in consequence of the indecision of the parties most interested, the burghers of the towns—an indecision into the causes of which we cannot here enter. From that moment the struggle degenerated into a fight between the local princes and the central power, and ended by blotting out Germany, for two hundred years, from the politically active nations of Europe. The Lutheran reformation produced a new creed indeed, a religion adapted to absolute monarchy. No sooner were the peasants of North-east Germany converted to Lutheranism than they were from freemen reduced to serfs.

But where Luther failed, Calvin won the day. Calvin's creed was one fit for the boldest of the bourgeoisie of his time. His predestination doctrine was the religious expression of the fact that in the commercial world of competition success or failure does not depend upon a man's activity or cleverness, but

upon circumstances uncontrollable by him. It is not
of him that willeth or of him that runneth, but of the
mercy of unknown superior economic powers; and
this was especially true at a period of economic revolution, when all old commercial routes and centres were
replaced by new ones, when India and America were
opened to the world, and when even the most sacred
economic articles of faith—the value of gold and silver
—began to totter and to break down. Calvin's church
constitution was thoroughly democratic and republican;
and where the kingdom of God was republicanised,
could the kingdoms of this world remain subject to
monarchs, bishops, and lords? While German Lutheranism became a willing tool in the hands of princes,
Calvinism founded a republic in Holland, and act've
republican parties in England, and, above all, Scotland.

In Calvinism, the second great bourgeois upheaval
found its doctrine ready cut and dried. This upheaval took place in England The middle-class of
the towns brought it on, and the yeomanry of the
country districts fought it out Curiously enough, in
all the three great bourgeois risings, the peasantry
furnishes the army that has to do the fighting; and
the peasantry is just the class that, the victory once
gained, is most surely ruined by the economic consequences of that victory A hundred years after
Cromwell, the yeomanry of England had almost
disappeared. Anyhow, had it not been for that
yeomanry and for the *plebeian* element in the towns,
the bourgeoisie alone would never have fought the

matter out to the bitter end, and would never have
brought Charles I. to the scaffold. In order to
secure even those conquests of the bourgeoisie that
were ripe for gathering at the time, the revolution
had to be carried considerably further—exactly as in
1793 in France and 1848 in Germany This seems,
in fact, to be one of the laws of evolution of bourgeois
society.

 Well, upon this excess of revolutionary activity
there necessarily followed the inevitable reaction
which in its turn went beyond the point where it
might have maintained itself. After a series of
oscillations, the new centre of gravity was at last
attained and became a new starting-point. The grand
period of English history, known to respectability
under the name of "the Great Rebellion," and the
struggles succeeding it, were brought to a close by
the comparatively puny event entitled by Liberal
historians, "the Glorious Revolution."

The new starting-point was a compromise between
the rising middle-class and the ex-feudal landowners.
The latter, though called, as now, the aristocracy, had
been long since on the way which led them to become what Louis Philippe in France became at a
much later period, "the first bourgeois of the kingdom." Fortunately for England, the old feudal
barons had killed one another during the Wars of
the Roses. Their successors, though mostly scions of
the old families, had been so much out of the direct
line of descent that they constituted quite a new
body, with habits and tendencies far more bourgeois

than feudal. They fully understood the value of money, and at once began to increase their rents by turning hundreds of small farmers out and replacing them by sheep. Henry VIII., while squandering the Church lands, created fresh bourgeois landlords by wholesale; the innumerable confiscations of estates, re-granted to absolute or relative upstarts, and continued during the whole of the seventeenth century, had the same result. Consequently, ever since Henry VII., the English "aristocracy," far from counteracting the development of industrial production, had, on the contrary, sought to indirectly profit thereby ; and there had always been a section of the great land-owners willing, from economical or political reasons, to co-operate with the leading men of the financial and industrial bourgeoisie. The compromise of 1689 was, therefore, easily accomplished. The political spoils of "pelf and place" were left to the great land-owning families, provided the economic interests of the financial, manufacturing, and commercial middle-class were sufficiently attended to And these economic interests were at that time powerful enough to determine the general policy of the nation. There might be squabbles about matters of detail, but, on the whole, the aristocratic oligarchy knew too well that its own economic prosperity was irretrievably bound up with that of the industrial and commercial middle-class.

From that time, the bourgeoisie was a humble, but still a recognised component of the ruling classes of England. With the rest of them, it had a common interest in keeping in subjection the great working mass of the nation. The merchant or manufacturer himself stood in the position of master, or, as it was until lately called, of "natural superior" to his clerks, his workpeople, his domestic servants. His interest was to get as much and as good work out of them as he could; for this end they had to be trained to proper submission. He was himself religious; his religion had supplied the standard under which he had fought the king and the lords; he was not long in discovering the opportunities this same religion offered him for working upon the minds of his natural inferiors, and making them submissive to the behests of the masters it had pleased God to place over them. In short, the English bourgeoisie now had to take a part in keeping down the "lower orders," the great producing mass of the nation, and one of the means employed for that purpose was the influence of religion.

There was another fact that contributed to strengthen the religious leanings of the bourgeoisie. That was the rise of materialism in England. This new doctrine not only shocked the pious feelings of the middle-class; it announced itself as a philosophy only fit for scholars and cultivated men of the world, in contrast to religion which was good enough for the uneducated masses, including the bourgeoisie. With Hobbes it stepped on the stage as a defender of royal prerogative and omnipotence; it called upon absolute monarchy to keep down that *puer robustus sed malitiosus*, to wit, the people. Similarly, with the

successors of Hobbes, with Bolingbroke, Shaftesbury,
etc., the new deistic form of materialism remained an
aristocratic, esoteric doctrine, and, therefore, hateful
to the middle-class both for its religious heresy and
for its anti-bourgeois political connexions. Accord-
ingly, in opposition to the materialism and deism of
the aristocracy, those Protestant sects which had furnished the flag and the fighting contingent against
the Stuarts, continued to furnish the main strength of
the progressive middle-class, and form even to-day
the backbone of " the Great Liberal Party."

In the meantime materialism passed from England
to France, where it met and coalesced with another
materialistic school of philosophers, a branch of
Cartesianism. In France, too, it remained at first an
exclusively aristocratic doctrine. But soon its revolutionary character asserted itself. The French
materialists did not limit their criticism to matters of
religious belief; they extended it to whatever scientific
tradition or political institution they met with; and
to prove the claim of their doctrine to universal application, they took the shortest cut, and boldly applied
it to all subjects of knowledge in the giant work
after which they were named—the *Encyclopédie.*
Thus, in one or the other of its two forms—avowed
materialism or deism—it became the creed of the
whole cultured youth of France; so much so that,
when the great Revolution broke out, the doctrine
hatched by English Royalists gave a theoretical flag
to French Republicans and Terrorists, and furnished
the text for the Declaration of the Rights of Man.

The great French Revolution was the third uprising of the bourgeoisie, but the first that had entirely cast off the religious cloak, and was fought out on undisguised political lines; it was the first, too, that was really fought out up to the destruction of one of the combatants, the aristocracy, and the complete triumph of the other, the bourgeoisie. In England the continuity of pre-revolutionary and post-revolutionary institutions, and the compromise between landlords and capitalists, found its expression in the continuity of judicial precedents and in the religious preservation of the feudal forms of the law. In France the Revolution constituted a complete breach with the traditions of the past; it cleared out the very last vestiges of feudalism, and created in the *Code Civil* a masterly adaptation of the old Roman law—that almost perfect expression of the juridical relations corresponding to the economic stage called by Marx the production of commodities—to modern capitalistic conditions; so masterly that this French revolutionary code still serves as a model for reforms of the law of property in all other countries, not excepting England. Let us, however, not forget that if English law continues to express the economic relations of capitalistic society in that barbarous feudal language which corresponds to the thing expressed, just as English spelling corresponds to English pronunciation—*vous écrivez Londres et vous prononcez Constantinople*, said a Frenchman—that same English law is the only one which has preserved through ages, and transmitted to America and the Colonies the best part of that old

Germanic personal freedom, local self-government, and independence from all interference but that of the law courts, which on the Continent has been lost during the period of absolute monarchy, and has nowhere been as yet fully recovered.

To return to our British bourgeois. The French Revolution gave him a splendid opportunity, with the help of the Continental monarchies, to destroy French maritime commerce, to annex French colonies, and to crush the last French pretensions to maritime rivalry. That was one reason why he fought it. Another was that the ways of this revolution went very much against his grain. Not only its "execrable" terrorism, but the very attempt to carry bourgeois rule to extremes. What should the British bourgeois do without his aristocracy, that taught him manners, such as they were, and invented fashions for him— that furnished officers for the army, which kept order at home, and the navy, which conquered colonial possessions and new markets abroad? There was indeed a progressive minority of the bourgeoisie, that minority whose interests were not so well attended to under the compromise; this section, composed chiefly of the less wealthy middle-class, did sympathise with the Revolution, but it was powerless in Parliament.

Thus, if materialism became the creed of the French Revolution, the God-fearing English bourgeois held all the faster to his religion. Had not the reign of terror in Paris proved what was the upshot, if the religious instincts of the masses were lost? The more materialism spread from France to neighbouring countries, and was reinforced by similar doctrinal currents, notably by German philosophy, the more, in fact, materialism and freethought generally became, on the Continent, the necessary qualifications of a cultivated man, the more stubbornly the English middle-class stuck to its manifold religious creeds. These creeds might differ from one another, but they were, all of them, distinctly religious, Christian creeds.

While the Revolution ensured the political triumph of the bourgeoisie in France, in England Watt, Arkwright, Cartwright, and others, initiated an industrial revolution, which completely shifted the centre of gravity of economic power. The wealth of the bourgeoisie increased considerably faster than that of the landed aristocracy. Within the bourgeoisie itself, the financial aristocracy, the bankers, etc., were more and more pushed into the background by the manufacturers. The compromise of 1689, even after the gradual changes it had undergone in favour of the bourgeoisie, no longer corresponded to the relative position of the parties to it. The character of these parties, too, had changed; the bourgeoisie of 1830 was very different from that of the preceding century. The political power still left to the aristocracy, and used by them to resist the pretensions of the new industrial bourgeoisie, became incompatible with the new economic interests. A fresh struggle with the aristocracy was necessary; it could end only in a victory of the new economic power. First, the Reform Act was pushed through, in spite of all resistance, under the impulse of the French Revolution of 1830. It gave to the bourgeoisie a recognised and powerful place in Parliament. Then the Repeal of the Corn Laws, which settled, once for all, the supremacy of the bourgeoisie, and especially of its most active portion, the manufacturers, over the landed aristocracy. This was the greatest victory of the bourgeoisie; it was, however, also the last it gained in its own exclusive interest. Whatever triumphs it obtained later on, it had to share with a new social power, first its ally, but soon its rival.

The industrial revolution had created a class of large manufacturing capitalists, but also a class—and a far more numerous one—of manufacturing work-people. This class gradually increased in numbers, in proportion as the industrial revolution seized upon one branch of manufacture after another, and in the same proportion it increased in power. This power it proved as early as 1824, by forcing a reluctant Parliament to repeal the acts forbidding combinations of workmen. During the Reform agitation, the working-men constituted the Radical wing of the Reform party; the Act of 1832 having excluded them from the suffrage, they formulated their demands in the People's Charter, and constituted themselves, in opposition to the great bourgeois Anti-Corn Law party, into an independent party, the Chartists, the first working-men's party of modern times.

Then came the Continental revolutions of February and March, 1848, in which the working people played such a prominent part, and, at least in Paris, put forward demands which were certainly inadmissible from the point of view of capitalist society. And then came the general reaction. First the defeat of the Chartists on the 10th April, 1848, then the crushing of the Paris working-men's insurrection in June of the same year, then the disasters of 1849 in Italy, Hungary, South Germany, and at last the victory of Louis Bonaparte over Paris, 2nd December, 1851. For a time, at least, the bugbear of working-class pretensions was put down, but' at what cost! If the British bourgeois had been convinced before of the necessity of maintaining the common people in a religious mood, how much more must' he feel that necessity after all these experiences? Regardless of the sneers of his Continental compeers, he continued to spend thousands and tens of thousands, year after year, upon the evangelisation of the lower orders; not content with his own native religious machinery, he appealed to Brother Jonathan, the greatest organiser in existence of religion as a trade, and imported from America revivalism, Moody and Sankey, and the like; and, finally, he accepted the dangerous aid of the Salvation Army, which revives the propaganda of early Christianity, appeals to the poor as the elect, fights capitalism in a religious way, and thus fosters an element of early Christian class antagonism, which one day may become troublesome to the well-to-do people who now find the ready money for it.

It seems a law of historical development that the bourgeoisie can in no European country get hold of political power—at least for any length of time—in

the same exclusive way in which the feudal aristocracy kept hold of it during the Middle Ages. Even
in France, where feudalism was completely extin-
guished, the bourgeoisie, as a whole, has held full
possession of the Government for very short periods
only. During Louis Philippe's reign, 1830-48, a very
small portion of the bourgeoisie ruled the kingdom;
by far the larger part were excluded from the suffrage
by the high qualification. Under the second Republic, 1848-51, the whole bourgeoisie ruled, but for
three years only; their incapacity brought on the
second Empire. It is only now, in the third Republic,
that the bourgeoisie as a whole have kept possession
of the helm for more than twenty years; and they
are already showing lively signs of decadence. A
durable reign of the bourgeoisie has been possible
only in countries like America, where feudalism was
unknown, and society at the very beginning started
from a bourgeois basis. And even in France and
America, the successors of the bourgeoisie, the working people, are already knocking at the door.

In England, the bourgeoisie never held undivided
sway. Even the victory of 1832 left the landed aristocracy in almost exclusive possession of all the
leading Government offices. The meekness with
which the wealthy middle-class submitted to this,
remained inconceivable to me until the great Liberal
manufacturer, Mr. W. A. Forster, in a public speech
implored the young men of Bradford to learn French,
as a means to get on in the world, and quoted from
his own experience how sheepish he looked when, as

a Cabinet Minister, he had to move in society where French was, at least, as necessary as English! The fact was, the English middle-class of that time were, as a rule, quite uneducated upstarts, and could not help leaving to the aristocracy those superior Government places where other qualifications were required than mere insular narrowness and insular conceit, seasoned by business sharpness.[1] Even now the endless newspaper debates about middle-class education show that the English middle-class does not yet con-

[1] And even in business matters, the conceit of national Chauvinism is but a sorry adviser. Up to quite recently, the average English manufacturer considered it derogatory from an Englishman to speak any language but his own, and felt rather proud than otherwise of the fact that "poor devils" of foreigners settled in England and took off his hands the trouble of disposing of his products abroad. He never noticed that these foreigners, mostly Germans, thus got command of a very large part of British foreign trade, imports and exports, and that the direct foreign trade of Englishmen became limited, almost entirely, to the colonies, China, the United States, and South America. Nor did he notice that these Germans traded with other Germans abroad, who gradually organised a complete network of commercial colonies all over the world. But when Germany, about forty years ago, seriously began manufacturing for export, this network served her admirably in her transformation, in so short a time, from a corn-exporting into a first-rate manufacturing country. Then, about ten years ago, the British manufacturer got frightened, and asked his ambassadors and consuls how it was that he could no longer keep his customers together. The unanimous answer was : (1) You don't learn your customer's language but expect him to speak your own; (2) You don't even try to suit your customer's wants, habits, and tastes, but expect him to conform to your English ones.

sider itself good enough for the best education, and
looks to something more modest. Thus, even after
the Repeal of the Corn Laws, it appeared a matter of
course, that the men who had carried the day, the
Cobdens, Brights, Forsters, etc., should remain excluded from a share in the official government of the
country, until twenty years afterwards, a new Reform
Act opened to them the door of the Cabinet. The
English bourgeoisie are, up to the present day, so
deeply penetrated by a sense of their social inferiority
that they keep up, at their own expense and that of
the nation, an ornamental caste of drones to represent the nation worthily at all State functions; and
they consider themselves highly honoured whenever
one of themselves is found worthy of admission into
this select and privileged body, manufactured, after
all, by themselves.

The industrial and commercial middle-class had,
therefore, not yet succeeded in driving the landed
aristocracy completely from political power when
another competitor, the working-class, appeared on
the stage. The reaction after the Chartist movement
and the Continental revolutions, as well as the unparalleled extension of English trade from 1848-1866,
(ascribed vulgarly to Free Trade alone, but due far more
to the colossal development of railways, ocean steamers,
and means of intercourse generally), had again driven
the working-class into the dependency of the Liberal
party, of which they formed, as in pre-Chartist times,
the Radical wing. Their claims to the franchise,
however, gradually became irresistible; while the

Whig leaders of the Liberals "funked," Disraeli showed his superiority by making the Tories seize the favourable moment and introduce household suffrage in the boroughs, along with a redistribution of seats. Then followed the ballot; then in 1884 the extension of household suffrage to the counties and a fresh redistribution of seats, by which electoral districts were to some extent equalised. All these measures considerably increased the electoral power of the working-class, so much so that in at least 150 to 200 constituencies that class now furnishes the majority of voters. But parliamentary government is a capital school for teaching respect for tradition; if the middle-class look with awe and veneration upon what Lord John Manners playfully called "our old nobility," the mass of the working-people then looked up with respect and deference to what used to be designated as "their betters," the middle-class. Indeed, the British workman, some fifteen years ago, was the model workman, whose respectful regard for the position of his master, and whose self-restraining modesty in claiming rights for himself, consoled our German economists of the *Katheder-Socialist* school for the incurable communistic and revolutionary tendencies of their own working-men at home.

But the English middle-class—good men of business as they are—saw farther than the German professors. They had shared their power but reluctantly with the working-class. They had learnt, during the Chartist years, what ·that *puer robustus sed malitiosus*, the people, is capable of. And since that time, they had been compelled to incorporate the better part of the People's Charter in the Statutes of the United Kingdom. Now, if ever, the people must be kept in order by moral means, and the first and foremost of all moral means of action upon the masses is and remains—religion. Hence the parsons' majorities on the School Boards, hence the increasing self-taxation of the bourgeoisie for the support of all sorts of revivalism, from ritualism to the Salvation Army.

And now came the triumph of British respectability over the freethought and religious laxity of the Continental bourgeois. The workmen of France and Germany had become rebellious. They were thoroughly infected with socialism, and, for very good reasons, were not at all particular as to the legality of the means by which to secure their own ascendency. The *puer robustus*, here, turned from day to day more *malitiosus*. Nothing remained to the French and German bourgeoisie as a last resource but to silently drop their freethought, as a youngster, when sea-sickness creeps upon him, quietly drops the burning cigar he brought swaggeringly on board; one by one, the scoffers turned pious in outward behaviour, spoke with respect of the Church, its dogmas and rites, and even conformed with the latter as far as could not be helped. French bourgeoisie dined *maigre* on Fridays, and German ones sat out long Protestant sermons in their pews on Sundays. They had come to grief with materialism. "*Die Religion muss dem Volk erhalten werden,*"—religion must be kept alive for the people— that was the only and the last means to save society from utter ruin. Unfortunately for themselves, they did not find this out until they had done their level best to break up religion for ever. And now it was the turn of the British bourgeois to sneer and to say: "Why, you fools, I could have told you that two hundred years ago!"

However, I am afraid neither the religious stolidity of the British, nor the *post festum* conversion of the Continental bourgeois will stem the rising Proletarian tide. Tradition is a great retarding force, is the *vis inertiæ* of history, but, being merely passive, is sure to be broken down; and thus religion will be no lasting safeguard to capitalist society. If our juridical, philosophical, and religious ideas are the more or less remote offshoots of the economical relations prevailing in a given society, such ideas cannot, in the long run, withstand the effects of a complete change in these relations. And, unless we believe in supernatural revelation, we must admit that no religious tenets will ever suffice to prop up a tottering society.

In fact, in England too, the working-people have begun to move again. They are, no doubt, shackled by traditions of various kinds. Bourgeois traditions, such as the widespread belief that there can be but two parties, Conservatives and Liberals, and that the working-class must work out its salvation by and through the great Liberal party. Working-men's traditions, inherited from their first tentative efforts at independent action, such as the exclusion, from ever so many old Trade Unions, of all applicants who have not gone through a regular apprenticeship; which means the breeding by every such union, of its own blacklegs. But for all that the English working-class is moving, as even Professor Brentano has sorrowfully had to report to his brother Katheder-Socialists. It moves, like all things in England, with a slow and measured step, with hesitation here, with more or less unfruitful, tentative attempts there ; it moves now and then with an over-cautious mistrust of the name of Socialism, while it gradually absorbs the substance ; and the movement spreads and seizes one layer of the workers after another. It has now shaken out of their torpor the unskilled labourers of the East End of London, and we all know what a splendid impulse these fresh forces have given it in return. And if the pace of the movement is not up to the impatience of some people, let them not forget that it is the working-class which keeps alive the finest qualities of the English character, and that, if a step in advance is once gained in England, it is, as a rule, never lost afterwards. If the sons of the old Chartists, for reasons explained above, were not quite up to the mark, the grandsons bid fair to be worthy of their forefathers.

But the triumph of the European working-class does not depend upon England alone. It can only be secured by the co-operation of, at least, England, France, and Germany. In both the latter countries the working-class movement is well ahead of England. In Germany it is even within measurable distance of success. The progress it has there made during the last twenty-five years is unparalleled. It advances with ever-increasing velocity. If the German middle-class have shown themselves lamentably deficient in political capacity, discipline, courage, energy, and perseverance, the German working-class have given ample proof of all these qualities. Four hundred years ago, Germany was the starting-point of the first upheaval of the European middle-class; as things are now, is it outside the limits of possibility that Germany will be the scene, too, of the first great victory of the European proletariat?

F. ENGELS.

April 20th, 1892.

SOCIALISM:
UTOPIAN AND SCIENTIFIC.

_____

I.

MODERN SOCIALISM IS, in its essence, the direct
product of the recognition, on the one hand, of
the class antagonisms, existing in the society
of to-day, between proprietors and non-pro-
prietors, between capitalists and wage-workers;
on the other hand, of the anarchy existing
in production. But, in its theoretical form,
modern Socialism originally appears ostensibly
as a more logical extension of the principles
laid down by the great French philosophers
of the eighteenth century. Like every new
theory, modern Socialism had, at first, to
connect itself with the intellectual stock-in-
trade ready to its hand, however deeply its
roots lay in material economic facts.

The great men, who in France prepared

A

men's minds for the coming revolution, were themselves extreme revolutionists. They recognised no external authority of any kind whatever. Religion, natural science, society, political institutions, everything, was subjected to the most unsparing criticism: everything must justify its existence before the judgment-seat of reason, or give up existence. Reason became the sole measure of everything. It was the time when, as Hegel says, the world stood upon its head;[1] first, in the sense that

[1] This is the passage on the French Revolution: " Thought, the concept of law, all at once made itself felt, and against this the old scaffolding of wrong could make no stand. In this conception of law, therefore, a constitution has now been established, and henceforth everything must be based upon this. Since the sun had been in the firmament, and the planets circled round him, the sight had never been seen of man standing upon his head—*i.e.*, on the Idea—and building reality after this image. Anaxagoras first said that the Nous, reason, rules the world; but now, for the first time, had man come to recognise that the Idea must rule the mental reality. And this was a magnificent sunrise. All thinking Beings have participated in celebrating this holy day. A sublime emotion swayed men at that time, an enthusiasm of reason pervaded the world, as if now had come the reconciliation of the Divine Principle with the world." [Hegel: " Philosophy of History," 1840,

the human head, and the principles arrived at by its thought, claimed to be the basis of all human action and association; but by and by, also, in the wider sense that the reality which was in contradiction to these principles had, in fact, to be turned upside down. Every form of society and government then existing, every old traditional notion was flung into the lumber-room as irrational; the world had hitherto allowed itself to be led solely by prejudices; everything in the past deserved only pity and contempt. Now, for the first time, appeared the light of day, the kingdom of reason; henceforth superstition, injustice, privilege, oppression. were to be superseded by eternal truth, eternal Right, equality based on Nature and the inalienable rights of man.

We know to-day that this kingdom of reason was nothing more than the idealised kingdom of the bourgeoisie; that this eternal Right found its realisation in bourgeois justice; that this equality reduced itself to bourgeois equality before the law; that bourgeois property was

p. 535.] Is it not high time to set the anti-Socialist law in action against such teachings, subversive and to the common danger, by the late Professor Hegel?

proclaimed as one of the essential rights of man; and that the government of reason, the Contrat Social of Rousseau, came into being, and only could come into being, as a democratic bourgeois republic. The great thinkers of the eighteenth century could, no more than their predecessors, go beyond the limits imposed upon them by their epoch.

But, side by side with the antagonism of the feudal nobility and the burghers, who claimed to represent all the rest of society, was the general antagonism of exploiters and exploited, of rich idlers and poor workers. It was this very circumstance that made it possible for the representatives of the bourgeoisie to put themselves forward as representing, not one special class, but the whole of suffering humanity. Still further. From its origin, the bourgeoisie was saddled with its antithesis: capitalists cannot exist without wage-workers, and, in the same proportion as the mediæval burgher of the guild developed into the modern bourgeois, the guild journeyman and the day-labourer, outside the guilds, developed into the proletarian. And although, upon the whole, the bourgeoisie, in their struggle with the nobility, could claim to represent at the same time the interests of the different working-classes of that period, yet in every great bourgeois movement there were independent outbursts of that class which was the forerunner, more or less developed, of the modern proletariat. For example, at the time of the German reformation and the peasants' war, the Anabaptists and Thomas Münzer; in the great English revolution, the Levellers; in the great French revolution, Babœuf.

There were theoretical enunciations corresponding with these revolutionary uprisings of a class not yet developed; in the sixteenth and seventeenth centuries, Utopian pictures of ideal social conditions; in the eighteenth, actual communistic theories (Morelly and Mably). The demand for equality was no longer limited to political rights; it was extended also to the social conditions of individuals. It was not simply class privileges that were to be abolished, but class distinctions themselves. A Communism, ascetic, denouncing all the pleasures of life, Spartan, was the first form of the new teaching. Then came the three great Utopians: Saint

Simon, to whom the middle-class movement, side by side with the proletarian, still had a certain significance; Fourier; and Owen, who in the country where capitalist production was most developed, and under the influence of the antagonisms begotten of this, worked out his proposals for the removal of class distinction systematically and in direct relation to French materialism.

One thing is common to all three. Not one of them appears as a representative of the interests of that proletariat, which historical development had, in the meantime, produced. Like the French philosophers, they do not claim to emancipate a particular class to begin with, but all humanity at once. Like them, they wish to bring in the kingdom of reason and eternal justice, but this kingdom, as they see it, is as far as heaven from earth, from that of the French philosophers.

For, to our three social reformers, the bourgeois world, based upon the principles of these philosophers, is quite as irrational and unjust, and, therefore, finds its way to the dust-hole quite as readily as feudalism and all the earlier stages of society. If pure reason and justice have not, hitherto, ruled

the world, this has been the case only because
men have not rightly understood them. What
was wanted was the individual man of genius,
who has now arisen and who understands the
truth. That he has now arisen, that the truth
has now been clearly understood, is not an
inevitable event, following of necessity in the
chain of historical development, but a mere
happy accident. He might just as well have
been born 500 years earlier, and might then
have spared humanity 500 years of error,
strife, and suffering.

We saw how the French philosophers of the
eighteenth century, the forerunners of the Revolution, appealed to reason as the sole judge
of all that is. A rational government, rational
society, were to be founded; everything that
ran counter to eternal reason was, to be remorselessly done away with. We saw also that
this eternal reason was in reality nothing but
the idealised understanding of the eighteenth
century citizen, just then evolving into the
bourgeois. The French Revolution had realised this rational society and government.

But the new order of things, rational enough
as compared with earlier conditions, turned

out to be by no means absolutely rational.
The State based upon reason completely
collapsed.   Rousseau's Contrat Social had
found its realisation in the Reign of Terror,
from which the bourgeoisie, who had lost con-
fidence in their own political capacity, had
taken refuge first in the corruption of the
Directorate, and, finally, under the wing of the
Napoleonic despotism. The promised eternal
peace was turned into an endless war of conquest.   The society based upon reason had
fared no better.   The antagonism between rich
and poor, instead of dissolving into general
prosperity, had become intensified by the removal of the guild and other privileges, which
had to some extent bridged it over, and by the
removal of the charitable institutions of the
Church.   The "freedom of property" from
feudal fetters, now veritably accomplished,
turned out to be, for the small capitalists and
small proprietors, the freedom to sell their
small property, crushed under the overmaster-
ing competition of the large capitalists and
landlords, to these great lords, and thus, as
far as the small capitalists and peasant proprietors were concerned, became "freedom

from property." The development of industry upon a capitalistic basis made poverty and misery of the working masses conditions of existence of society. Cash payment became more and more, in Carlyle's phrase, the sole nexus between man and man. The number of crimes increased from year to year. Formerly, the feudal vices had openly stalked about in broad daylight ; though not eradicated, they were now at any rate thrust into the background. In their stead, the bourgeois vices, hitherto practised in secret, began to blossom all the more luxuriantly. Trade became to a greater and greater extent cheating. The " fraternity " of the revolutionary motto was realised in the chicanery and rivalries of the battle of competition. Oppression by force was replaced by corruption ; the sword, as the first social lever, by gold. The right of the first night was transferred from the feudal lords to the bourgeois manufacturers. Prostitution increased to an extent never heard of. Marriage itself remained, as before, the legally recognised form, the official cloak of prostitution, and, moreover, was supplemented by rich crops of adultery.

In a word, compared with the splendid
promises of the philosophers, the social and
political institutions born of the "triumph of
reason" were bitterly disappointing carica-
tures. All that was wanting was the men to
formulate this disappointment, and they came
with the turn of the century. In 1802 Saint
Simon's Geneva letters appeared; in 1808
appeared Fourier's first work, although the
groundwork of his theory dated from 1799;
on January 1, 1800, Robert Owen undertook
the direction of New Lanark.

At this time, however, the capitalist mode
of production, and with it the antagonism between the bourgeoisie and the proletariat, was
still very incompletely developed. Modern
Industry, which had just arisen in England,
was still unknown in France. But Modern
Industry develops, on the one hand, the
conflicts which make absolutely necessary a
revolution in the mode of production, and the
doing away with its capitalistic character—conflicts not only between the classes begotten of
it, but also between the very productive forces
and the forms of exchange created by it. And,
on the other hand, it develops, in these very

gigantic productive forces, the means of ending
these conflicts. If, therefore, about the year
1800, the conflicts arising from the new social
order were only just beginning to take shape,
this holds' still more fully as to the means of
ending them. The "have-nothing" masses of
Paris, during the Reign of Terror, were able for
a moment to gain the mastery, and thus to lead
the bourgeois revolution to victory in spite of
the bourgeoisie themselves.   But, in doing so,
they only proved how impossible it was for
their domination to last under the conditions
then obtaining. The proletariat, which then for
the first time evolved itself from these "have-
nothing" masses as the nucleus of a new class,
as yet quite incapable of independent political
action, appeared as an oppressed, suffering
order, to whom, in its incapacity to help itself,
help could, at best, be brought in from without,
or down from above.

   This historical situation also dominated the
founders of Socialism. To the crude conditions
of capitalistic production and the crude class
conditions corresponded crude theories. The
solution of the social problems, which as yet
lay hidden in undeveloped economic conditions,

the Utopians attempted to evolve out of the
human brain. Society presented nothing but
wrongs, to remove these was the task of reason.
It was necessary, then, to discover a new and
more perfect system of social order and to im-
pose this upon society from without by propaganda, and, wherever it was possible, by the
example of model experiments. These new
social systems were foredoomed as Utopian; the
more completely they were worked out in detail,
the more they could not avoid drifting off into
pure phantasies.

These facts once established, we need not
dwell a moment longer upon this side of the
question, now wholly belonging to the past. We
can leave it to the literary small fry to solemnly
quibble over these phantasies, which to-day only
make us smile, and to crow over the superiority
of their own bald reasoning, as compared with
such "insanity." For ourselves, we delight in
the stupendously grand thoughts and germs of
thought that everywhere break out through
their phantastic covering, and to which these
Philistines are blind.

Saint Simon was a son of the great French
Revolution, at the outbreak of which he was not

yet thirty. The Revolution was the victory of the third estate, *i.e.*, of the great masses of the nation, *working* in production and in trade, over the privileged *idle* classes, the nobles and the priests. But the victory of the third estate soon revealed itself as exclusively the victory of a small part of this "estate," as the conquest of political power by the socially privileged section of it, *i.e.*, the propertied bourgeoisie. And the bourgeoisie had certainly developed rapidly during the Revolution, partly by speculation in the lands of the nobility and of the Church, confiscated and afterwards put up for sale, and partly by frauds upon the nation by means of army contracts. It was the domination of these swindlers that, under the Directorate, brought France to the verge of ruin, and thus gave Napoleon the pretext for his *coup-d'état.*

Hence, to Saint Simon the antagonism between the third estate and the privileged classes took the form of an antagonism between "workers" and "idlers." The idlers were not merely the old privileged classes, but also all who, without taking any part in production or distribution, lived on their incomes. And the workers were not only the wage-workers, but

also the manufacturers, the merchants, the
bankers. That the idlers had lost the capacity
for intellectual leadership and political supremacy
had been proved, and was by the Revolution
finally settled. That the non-possessing classes
had not this capacity seemed to Saint Simon
proved by the experiences of the Reign of
Terror. Then, who was to lead and command? According to Saint Simon, science
and industry, both united by a new religious
bond, destined to restore that unity of religious
ideas which had been lost since the time of the
Reformation—a necessarily mystic and rigidly
hierarchic "new Christianity." But science, that
was the scholars; and industry, that was, in the
first place, the working bourgeois, manufacturers,
merchants, bankers. These bourgeoisie were,
certainly, intended by Saint Simon to transform
themselves into a kind of public officials, of social
trustees; but they were still to hold, *vis-à-vis* of
the workers, a commanding and economically
privileged position. The bankers especially
were to be called upon to direct the whole of
social production by the regulation of credit.
This conception was in exact keeping with a
time in which Modern Industry in France and,

with it, the chasm between bourgeoisie and proletariat was only just coming into existence. But what Saint Simon especially lays stress upon is this : what interests him first, and above all other things, is the lot of the class that is the most numerous and the most poor *("la classe la plus nombreuse et la plus pauvre")*.

Already, in his Geneva letters, Saint Simon lays down the proposition that "all men ought to work." In the same work he recognises also that the Reign of Terror was the reign of the non-possessing masses. "See," says he to them, "what happened in France at the time when your comrades held sway there ; they brought about a famine." But to recognise the French Revolution as a class war, and not simply one between nobility and bourgeoisie, but between nobility, bourgeoisie, and the non-possessors, was, in the year 1802, a most pregnant discovery. In 1816, he declares that politics is the science of production, and foretells the complete absorption of politics by economics. The knowledge that economic conditions are the basis of political institutions appears here only in embryo. Yet what is here already very plainly expressed is the idea of the

future conversion of political rule over men into
an administration of things and a direction of
processes of production—that is to say, the
"abolition of the State," about which recently
there has been so much noise.

Saint Simon shows the same superiority over
his contemporaries, when in 1814, immediately
after the entry of the allies into Paris, and again
in 1815, during the Hundred Days' War, he
proclaims the alliance of France with England, and then of both these countries with
Germany, as the only guarantee for the pros-
perous development and peace of Europe. To
preach to the French in 1815 an alliance with
the victors of Waterloo required as much
courage as historical foresight.

If in Saint Simon we find a comprehensive
breadth of view, by virtue of which almost all
the ideas of later Socialists, that are not strictly
economic, are found in him in embryo, we find
in Fourier a criticism of the existing conditions of society, genuinely French and witty,
but not upon that account any the less thor-
ough. Fourier takes the bourgeoisie, their
inspired prophets before the Revolution, and
their interested eulogists after it, at their own

word. He lays bare remorselessly the material and moral misery of the bourgeois world. He confronts it with the earlier philosophers' dazzling promises of a society in which reason alone should reign, of a civilisation in which happiness should be universal, of an illimitable human perfectibility, and with the rose-coloured phraseology of the bourgeois ideologists of his time. He points out how everywhere the most pitiful reality corresponds with the most high-sounding phrases, and he overwhelms this hopeless fiasco of phrases with his mordant sarcasm.

Fourier is not only a critic; his imperturbably serene nature makes him a satirist, and assuredly one of the greatest satirists of all time. He depicts, with equal power and charm, the swindling speculations that blossomed out upon the downfall of the Revolution, and the shopkeeping spirit prevalent in, and characteristic of, French commerce at that time. Still more masterly is his criticism of the bourgeois form of the relations between the sexes, and the position of woman in bourgeois society. He was the first to declare that in any given society the degree

B

of woman's emancipation is the natural measure
of the general emancipation.

But Fourier is at his greatest in his conception of the history of society. He divides
its whole course, thus far, into four stages of
evolution—savagery, barbarism, the patriarch-
ate, civilisation. This last is identical with the
so-called civil, or bourgeois, society of to-day—
i.e., with the social order that came in with the
sixteenth century. He proves "that the civilised stage raises every vice practised by
barbarism in a simple fashion, into a form of
existence, complex, ambiguous, equivocal, hy-
pocritical"—that civilisation moves in "a vicious
circle," in contradictions which it constantly re-
produces without being able to solve them; hence
it constantly arrives at the very opposite to that
which it wants to attain, or pretends to want to
attain, so that, *e.g.*, "under civilisation poverty
is born of superabundance itself."

Fourier, as we see, uses the dialectic method
in the same masterly way as his contemporary,
Hegel. Using these same dialectics, he argues,
against the talk about illimitable human perfectibility, that every historical phase has its
period of ascent and also its period of descent,

and he applies this observation to the future of the whole human race. As Kant introduced into natural science the idea of the ultimate destruction of the earth, Fourier introduced into historical science that of the ultimate destruction of the human race.

.r Whilst in France the hurricane of the Revolution swept over the land, in England a quieter, but not on that account less tremendous, revolution was going on. Steam and the new tool - making machinery were transforming manufacture into modern industry, and thus revolutionising the whole foundation of bourgeois society. The sluggish march of development of the manufacturing period changed into a veritable storm and stress period of production. With constantly increasing swiftness the splitting-up of society into large capitalists and non-possessing proletarians went on. Between these, instead of the former stable middle-class, an unstable mass of artisans and small shopkeepers, the most fluctuating portion of the population, now led a precarious existence.

The new mode of production was, as yet, only at the beginning of its period of ascent; as yet it was the normal, regular method of pro-

duction—the only one possible under existing
conditions.　Nevertheless, even then it was
producing crying social abuses—the herding
together of a homeless population in the worst
quarters of the large towns ; the loosening of
all traditional moral bonds, of patriarchal subordination, of family relations ; overwork, especially of women and children, to a frightful
extent ; complete demoralisation of the working-class, suddenly flung into altogether new
conditions, from· the country into the town,
from agriculture into modern industry, from
stable conditions of existence into insecure
ones that changed from day to day.

At this juncture there came forward as a
reformer a manufacturer 29 years old—a man
of almost sublime, childlike simplicity of character, and at the same time one of the few
born leaders of men.　Robert Owen had
adopted the teaching of the materialistic
philosophers : that man's character is the product, on the one hand, of heredity, on the
other, of the environment of the individual
during his lifetime, and especially during his
period of development.　In the industrial revolution most of his class saw only chàos and

confusion, and the opportunity of fishing in these troubled waters and making large fortunes quickly. He saw in it the opportunity of putting into practice his favourite theory, and so of bringing order out of chaos. He had already tried it with success, as superintendent of more than five hundred men in a Manchester factory. From 1800 to 1829, he directed the great cotton mill at New Lanark, in Scotland, as managing partner, along the same lines, but with greater freedom of action and with a success that made him a European reputation. A population, originally consisting of the most diverse and, for the most part, very demoralised elements, a population that gradually grew to 2,500, he turned into a model colony, in which drunkenness, police, magistrates, lawsuits, poor laws, charity, were unknown. And all this simply by placing the people in conditions worthy of human beings, and especially by carefully bringing up the rising generation. He was the founder of infant schools, and introduced them first at New Lanark. At the age of two the children came to school, where they enjoyed themselves so much that they could scarcely be got home again. Whilst his

competitors worked their people thirteen or
fourteen hours a day, in New Lanark the
working-day was only ten and a half hours.
When a crisis in cotton stopped work for four
months, his workers received their full wages
all the time. And with all this the business
more. than doubled in value, and to the last
yielded large profits to its proprietors.

In spite of all this, Owen was not content.
The existence which he secured for his workers
was, in his eyes, still far from being worthy of
human beings. "The people were slaves at
my mercy." The relatively favourable conditions in which he had placed them were still
far from allowing a rational development of
the character and of the intellect in all direc-
tions, much less of the free exercise of all
their faculties. "And yet, the working part
of this population of 2500 persons was daily
producing as much real wealth for society as,
less than half a century before, it would have
required the working part of a population of
600,000 to create. I asked myself, what became of the difference between the wealth
consumed by 2500 persons and that which
would have been consumed by 600,000?"[1]

[1] From "The Revolution in Mind and Practice," p. 21.

The answer was clear. It had been used to pay the proprietors of the establishment 5 per cent. on the capital they had laid out, in addition to over £300,000 clear profit. And that which held for New Lanark held to a still greater extent for all the factories in England. " If this new wealth had not been created by machinery, imperfectly as it has been applied, the wars of Europe, in opposition to Napoleon, and to support the aristocratic principles of society, could not have been maintained. And yet this new power was the creation of the working-classes."[1] To them, therefore, the fruits of this new power belonged. The newly - created gigantic productive . forces, hitherto used only to enrich individuals and to enslave the masses, offered to Owen the foundations for a reconstruction of society; they were destined, as the common property of all, to be worked for the common good of all.

Owen's Communism was based upon this

a memorial addressed to all the "red Republicans, Communists and Socialists of Europe," and sent to the provisional government of France, 1848, and also "to Queen Victoria and her responsible advisers."

[1] Note, l. c., p. 22.

purely business foundation, the outcome, so to
say, of commercial calculation. Throughout,
it maintained this practical character. Thus,
in 1823, Owen proposed the relief of the distress
in Ireland by Communist colonies, and drew up
complete estimates of costs of founding them,
yearly expenditure, and probable revenue.
And in his definite plan for the future, the
technical working out of details is managed
with such practical knowledge—ground plan,
front and side and bird's-eye views all included
—that the Owen method of social reform once
accepted, there is from the practical point of
view little to be said against the actual arrangement of details.

His advance in the direction of Communism
was the turning-point in Owen's life. As
long as he was simply a philanthropist, he was
rewarded with nothing but wealth, applause,
honour, and glory. He was the most popular
man in Europe. Not only men of his own
class, but statesmen and princes listened to
him approvingly. But when he came out
with his Communist theories, that was quite
another thing. Three great obstacles seemed
to him especially to block the path to social

reform : private property, religion, the present form of marriage. He knew what confronted him if he attacked these—outlawry, excommunication from official society, the loss of his whole social position. But nothing of this prevented him from attacking them without fear of consequences, and what he had foreseen happened. Banished from official society, with a conspiracy of silence against him in the press, ruined by his unsuccessful Communist experiments in America, in which he sacrificed all his fortune, he turned directly to the working-class and continued working in their midst for thirty years. Every social movement, every real advance in England on behalf of the workers links itself on to the name of Robert Owen. He forced through in 1819, after five years' fighting, the first law limiting the hours of labour of women and children in factories. He was president of the first Congress at which all the Trade Unions of England united in a single great trade association. He introduced as transition measures to the complete communistic organisation of society, on the one hand, co-operative societies for retail trade and production. These have since that time, at least, given

practical proof that the merchant and the manufacturer are socially quite unnecessary. On
the other hand, he introduced labour bazaars
for the exchange of the products of labour
through the medium of labour-notes, whose
unit was a single hour of work; institutions
necessarily doomed to failure, but completely
anticipating Proudhon's bank of exchange of a
much later period, and differing entirely from
this in that it did not claim to be the panacea
for all social ills, but only a first step towards
a much more radical revolution of society.

The Utopians' mode of thought has for a
long time governed the socialist ideas of the
nineteenth century, and still governs some of
them. Until very recently all French and
English Socialists did homage to it. The
earlier German Communism, including that of
Weitling, was of the same school. To all
these Socialism is the expression of absolute truth, reason, and justice, and has only
to be discovered to conquer all the world by
virtue of its own power. And as absolute
truth is independent of time, space, and of the
historical development of man, it is a mere
accident when and where it is discovered.

With all this, absolute truth, reason, and justice are different with the founder of each different school. And as each one's special kind of absolute truth, reason, and justice is again conditioned by his subjective understanding, his conditions of existence, the measure of his knowledge and his intellectual training, there is no other ending possible in this conflict of absolute truths than that they shall be mutually exclusive one of the other. Hence, from this nothing could come but a kind of eclectic, average Socialism, which, as a matter of fact, has up to the present time dominated the minds of most of the socialist workers in France and England. Hence, a mish-mash allowing of the most manifold shades of opinion; a mish-mash of such critical statements, economic theories, pictures of future society by the founders of different sects, as excite a minimum of opposition; a mish-mash which is the more easily brewed, the more the definite sharp edges of the individual constituents are rubbed down in the stream of debate, like rounded pebbles in a brook.

To make a science of Socialism, it had first to be placed upon a real basis.

II.

In the meantime, along with and after the French philosophy of the eighteenth century had arisen the new German philosophy, culminating in Hegel. Its greatest merit was the taking up again of dialectics as the highest form of reasoning. The old Greek philosophers were all born natural dialecticians, and Aristotle, the most encyclopædic intellect of them, had already analysed the most essential forms of dialectic thought. The newer philosophy, on the other hand, although in it also dialectics had brilliant exponents (*e.g.* Descartes and Spinoza), had, especially through English influence, become more and more rigidly fixed in the so-called metaphysical mode of reasoning, by which also the French of the eighteenth century were almost wholly dominated, at all events in their special philosophical work. Outside philosophy in the restricted sense, the French nevertheless produced masterpieces of dialectic. We need only call to mind Diderot's "Le Neveu de Rameau," and Rousseau's "Discours sur l'origine et les fondements de l'inégalité parmi les hommes." We give here, in brief, the essential character of these two modes of thought.

When we consider and reflect upon nature at large, or the history of mankind, or our own intellectual activity, at first we see the picture of an endless entanglement of relations and reactions, permutations and combinations, in which nothing remains what, where, and as it was, but everything moves, changes, comes into being and passes away. We see, therefore, at first the picture as a whole, with its individual parts still more or less kept in the background; we observe the movements, transitions, connections, rather than the things that move, combine, and are connected. This primitive, naïve, but intrinsically correct conception of the world is that of ancient Greek philosophy, and was first clearly formulated by Heraclitus: everything is and is not, for everything is fluid, is constantly changing, constantly coming into being and passing away.

But this conception, correctly as it expresses the general character of the picture of appear-

ances as a whole, does not suffice to explain the
details of which this picture is made up, and so
long as we do not understand these, we have
not a clear idea of the whole picture. In order
to understand these details we must detach
them from their natural or historical connection
and examine each one separately, its nature,
special causes, effects, etc. This is, primarily,
the task of natural science and historical research; branches of science which the Greeks
of classical times, on very good grounds, rel-
egated to a subordinate position, because they
had first of all to collect materials for these
sciences to work upon. A certain amount of
natural and historical material must be collected
before there can be any critical analysis, comparison, and arrangement in classes, orders, and
species. The foundations of the exact natural
sciences were, therefore, first worked out by
the Greeks of the Alexandrian period, and later
on, in the Middle Ages, by the Arabs. Real
natural science dates from the second half of
the fifteenth century, and thence onward it has
advanced with constantly increasing rapidity.
The analysis of Nature into its individual parts,
the grouping of the different natural processes

and objects in definite classes, the study of the
internal anatomy of organised bodies in their
manifold forms—these were the fundamental
conditions of the gigantic strides in our knowledge of Nature that have been made during
the last four hundred years. But this method
of work has also left us as legacy the habit of
observing natural objects and processes in
isolation, apart from their connection with the
vast whole; of observing them in repose, not
in motion; as constants, not as essentially
variables; in their death, not in their life.
And when this way of looking at things was
transferred by Bacon and Locke from natural
science to philosophy, it begot the narrow,
metaphysical mode of thought peculiar to
the last century.

To the metaphysician, things and their
mental reflexes, ideas, are isolated, are to be
considered one after the other and apart from
each other, are objects of investigation fixed,
rigid, given once for all. He thinks in absolutely irreconcilable antitheses. " His communication is 'yea, yea; nay, nay;' for what-
soever is more than these cometh of evil."
For him a thing either exists or does not exist;

a thing cannot at the same time be itself and something' else.　Positive and negative absolutely exclude one another; cause and effect stand in a rigid antithesis one to the other.

At first sight this mode of thinking seems to us very luminous, because it is that of so-called sound commonsense.　Only sound commonsense, respectable fellow that he is, in the homely realm of his own four walls, has very wonderful adventures directly he ventures out into the wide world of research.　And the metaphysical mode of thought, justifiable and necessary as it is in a number of domains whose extent varies according to the nature of the particular object of investigation, sooner or later reaches a limit, beyond which it becomes one-sided, restricted, abstract, lost in insoluble contradictions. In the contemplation of individual things, it forgets the connection between them; in the contemplation of their existence, it forgets the beginning and end of that existence; of their repose, it forgets their motion.　It cannot see the wood for the trees.

For everyday purposes we know and can say, *e.g.*, whether an animal is alive or not.　But, upon closer inquiry, we find that this is, in

many cases, a very complex question, as the
jurists know very well. They have cudgelled
their brains in vain to discover a rational limit
beyond which the killing of the child in its
mother's womb is murder. It is just as impossible to determine absolutely the moment of
death, for physiology proves that death is not
an instantaneous, momentary phenomenon, but
a very protracted process.

In like manner, every organised being is
every moment the same and not the same;
every moment it assimilates matter supplied
from without, and gets rid of other matter; every
moment some cells of its body die and others
build themselves anew; in a longer or shorter
time the matter of its body is completely
renewed, and is replaced by other molecules of
matter, so that every organised being is always
itself, and yet something other than itself.

Further, we find upon closer investigation
that the two poles of an antithesis, positive
and negative, *e.g.*, are as inseparable as they
are opposed, and that despite all their opposition,
they mutually interpenetrate. And we find, in
like manner, that cause and effect are concep-
tions which only hold good in their application

to individual cases, but as soon as we consider
the individual cases in their general connection
with the universe as a whole, they run into each
other, and they become confounded when we
contemplate that universal action and reaction in
which causes and effects are eternally changing
places, so that what is effect here and now will
be cause there and then, and *vice versa.*

None of these processes and modes of
thought enters into the framework of metaphysical reasoning.   Dialectics, on the other
hand, comprehends things and their representations, ideas, in their essential connection,
concatenation, motion, origin, and ending.
Such processes as those mentioned above are,
therefore, so many corroborations of its own
method of procedure.

Nature is the proof of dialectics, and it must
be said for modern science that it has furnished
this proof with very rich materials increasing
daily, and thus has shown that, in the last
resort, Nature works dialectically and not
metaphysically ; that she does not move in the
eternal oneness of a perpetually recurring circle,
but goes through a real historical evolution.
In this connection Darwin must be named

before all others. He dealt the metaphysical conception of Nature the heaviest blow by his proof that all organic beings, plants, animals, and man himself, are the products of a process of evolution going on through millions of years. But the naturalists who have learned to think dialectically are few and far between, and this conflict of the results of discovery with preconceived modes of thinking explains the endless confusion now reigning in theoretical natural science, the despair of teachers as well as learners, of authors and readers alike.

An exact representation of the universe, of its evolution, of the development of mankind, and of the reflection of this evolution in the minds of men, can therefore only be obtained by the methods of dialectics with its constant regard to the innumerable actions and reactions of life and death, of progressive or retrogressive changes. And in this spirit the new German philosophy has worked. Kant began his career by resolving the stable solar system of Newton and its eternal duration, after the famous initial impulse had once been given, into the result of a historic process, the formation of the sun and all the planets out of a rotating nebulous mass. From this he at the same time drew the conclusion that, given this origin of the solar system, its future death followed of necessity. His theory half a century later was established mathe-matically ·by Laplace, and half. a century after that the spectroscope proved the existence in space of such incandescent masses of gas in various stages of condensation.

This new German philosophy culminated in the Hegelian system. In this system—and herein is its great merit—for the first time the whole world. natural, historical, intellectual, is represented as a process, *i.e* , as in constant motion. change. transformation, development , and the attempt is made to trace out the internal connection that makes a continuous whole of all this movement and development. From this point of view the history of man-kind no longer appeared as a wild whirl of senseless deeds of violence. all equally con-demnable at the judgment seat of mature philosophic reason, and which are best forgotten as quickly as possible; but as the process of evolution of man himself. It was now the task of the intellect to follow the gradual march of this process through all its devious ways, and to trace out the inner law running through all its apparently accidental phenomena.

That the Hegelian system did not solve the problem it propounded is here ·immaterial. Its epoch-making merit was that it propounded the problem. This:problem is one that no single individual will ever be able to solve. Although Hegel was—with Saint Simon—the most en-cyclopædic mind of his time, yet he was limited, first, by the necessarily limited extent of his own knowledge, and, second, by the limited extent and depth of the knowledge and con-ceptions of his.age. To' these limits a third must be added. Hegel was an idealist. To. him the thoughts within his brain were not the more or less abstract pictures of actual things and processes, but, conversely, things and their evolution were only the realised pictures of the "Idea," existing somewhere from eternity before the world was. This way of thinking turned everything upside down, and completely reversed the actual connection of things in the world. Correctly and ingeniously as many individual groups of facts were 'grasped by Hegel, yet, for the reasons just given, there is much that is botched, artificial, laboured, in

a word, wrong in point of detail. The
Hegelian system, in itself, was a colossal mis-
carriage—but it was also the last of its kind.
It was suffering, in fact, from an internal
and incurable contradiction.   Upon the one
hand, its essential proposition was the conception that human history is a process of
evolution, which, by its very nature, cannot
find its intellectual final term in the discovery
of any so-called absolute truth.   But, on the
other hand, it laid claim to being the very
essence of this absolute truth.   A system of
natural and historical knowledge, embracing
everything, and final for all time, is a contradiction to the fundamental law of dialectic
reasoning.   This law, indeed, by no means
excludes, but, on the contrary, includes the
idea that the systematic knowledge of the
external universe can make giant strides from
age to age.

The perception of the fundamental contradiction in German idealism led necessarily back
to materialism, but *nota bene*, not to the simply
metaphysical, exclusively mechanical materialism of the eighteenth century.   Old materialism
looked upon all previous history as a crude heap

of irrationality and violence; modern materialism sees in it the process of evolution of
humanity, and aims at discovering the laws
thereof. With the French of the eighteenth
century, and even with Hegel, the conception
obtained of Nature as a whole, moving in
narrow circles, and forever immutable, with its
eternal celestial bodies, as Newton, and unalterable organic species, as Linnæus, taught.
Modern materialism embraces the more recent
discoveries of natural science, according to
which Nature also has its history in time, the
celestial bodies, like the organic species that,
under favourable conditions, people them, being
born and perishing. And even if Nature, as a
whole, must still be said to move in recurrent
cycles, these cycles assume infinitely larger
dimensions. In both aspects, modern materialism is essentially dialectic, and no longer requires the assistance of that sort of philosophy
which, queen-like, pretended to rule the remaining mob of sciences. As soon as each special
science is bound to make clear its position in the
great totality of things and of our knowledge
of things, a special science dealing with this
totality is superfluous or unnecessary. That

which still survives of all earlier philosophy is
the science of thought and its laws—formal logic
and dialectics.   Everything else is subsumed
in the positive science of Nature and history.

Whilst, however, the revolution in the conception of Nature could only be made in proportion to the corresponding positive materials
furnished by research, already much earlier
certain historical facts had occurred which led
to a decisive change in the conception of history.   In 1831, the first working-class rising
took place in Lyons ; between 1838 and 1842,
the first national working-class movement, that
of the English Chartists, reached its height.
The class struggle between proletariat and
bourgeoisie came to the front in the history
of the most advanced countries in Europe, in
proportion to the development, upon the one
hand, of modern industry, upon the other,
of the newly-acquired political supremacy of
the bourgeoisie.   Facts more and more strenu-
ously gave the lie to the teachings of bourgeois
economy as to the identity of the interests of
capital and labour, as to the universal harmony
and universal prosperity that would be the
consequence of unbridled competition.   All

these things could no longer be ignored, any more than the French and English Social- ism, which was their theoretical, though very imperfect, expression. But the old idealist conception of history, which was not yet dis- lodged, knew nothing of class struggles based upon economic interests, knew nothing of eco- nomic interests; production and all economic relations appeared in it only as incidental, sub- ordinate elements in the "history of civilisation."

The new facts made imperative a new ex- amination of all past history Then it was seen that *all* past history, with the exception of its primitive stages, was the history of class struggles; that these warring classes of society are always the products of the modes of pro- duction and of exchange—in a word, of the *economic* conditions of their time; that the economic structure of society always furnishes the real basis, starting from which we can alone work out the ultimate explanation of the whole superstructure of juridical and political institutions as well as of the religious, philosophical, and other ideas of a given historical period. Hegel had freed his- tory from metaphysics—he had made it dialectic; but his conception of history was essentially idealistic. But now idealism was driven from its last refuge, the philosophy of history; now a materialistic treatment of history was propounded, and a method found of explaining man's "knowing" by his "being," instead of, as heretofore, his "being" by his "knowing."

From that time forward Socialism was no longer an accidental discovery of this or that ingenious brain, but the necessary outcome of the struggle between two historically developed classes—the proletariat and the bourgeoisie. Its task was no longer to manufacture a system of society as perfect as possible, but to examine the historico-economic succession of events from which these classes and their antagonism had of necessity sprung, and to discover in the economic conditions thus created the means of ending the conflict. But the Socialism of earlier days was as incompatible with this materialistic conception as the conception of Nature of the French materialists was with dialectics and modern natural science. The Socialism of earlier days certainly criticised the existing capitalistic mode of production and its consequences. But it could not

explain them, and, therefore, could not get the
mastery of them. It could only simply reject
them as bad. ·The more strongly this earlier
Socialism denounced the exploitation of the
working-class, inevitable under Capitalism, the
less able was it clearly to show in what this
exploitation consisted and how it arose. But
for this it was necessary—(1) to present the
capitalistic method of production in its historical
connection and its inevitableness during a
particular historical period, and therefore, also,
to present its inevitable downfall; and (2) to
lay bare its essential character, which was still
a secret. This was done by the discovery of
surplus-value. It was shown that the appropriation of unpaid labour is the basis of the
capitalist mode of production and of the exploitation of the worker that occurs under it;
that even if the capitalist buys the labour-power
of his labourer at its full value as a commodity
on the market, he yet extracts more value from
it than he paid for; and that in the ultimate
analysis this surplus-value forms those sums of
value from which are heaped up the constantly
increasing masses of capital in the hands of the
possessing classes. The genesis of capitalist

production and the production of capital were both explained.

These two great discoveries, the materialistic conception of history and the revelation of the secret of capitalistic production through surplus-value, we owe to Marx. With these discoveries Socialism became a science. The next thing was to work out all its details and relations.

III.

THE materialist conception of history starts from the proposition that the production of the means to support human life and, next to production, the exchange of things produced, is the basis of all social structure; that in every society that has appeared in history, the manner in which wealth is distributed and society divided into classes or orders, is dependent upon what is produced, how it is produced, and how the products are exchanged. From this point of view the final causes of all social changes and political revolutions are to be sought, not in men's brains, not in man's better insight into eternal truth and justice, but in changes in the modes of production and exchange. They are to be sought, not in the *philosophy*, but in the *economics* of each particular epoch. The growing perception that existing social institutions are unreasonable and unjust, that reason has become unreason, and right wrong, is only proof that in the modes of production and exchange

changes have silently taken place, with which
the social order, adapted to earlier economic
conditions, is no longer in keeping. From this
it also follows that the means of getting rid of
the incongruities that have been brought to
light, must also be present, in a more or less
developed condition, within the changed modes
of production themselves. These means are not
to be invented by deduction from fundamental
principles, but are to be discovered in the stub-
born facts of the existing system of production.

What is, then, the position of modern
Socialism in this connexion?

The present structure of society—this is now
pretty generally conceded—is the creation of the
ruling class of to-day, of the bourgeoisie. The
mode of production peculiar to the bourgeoisie, known, since Marx, as the capitalist
mode of production, was incompatible with the
feudal system, with the privileges it conferred
upon individuals, entire social ranks and local
corporations, as well as with the hereditary ties
of subordination which constituted the framework
of its social organisation. The bourgeoisie broke
up the feudal system and built upon its ruins the
capitalist order of society, the kingdom of free

competition, of personal liberty, of the equality, before the law, of all commodity owners, of all the rest of the capitalist blessings. Thenceforward the capitalist mode of production could develop in freedom. Since steam, machinery, and the making of machines by machinery transformed the older manufacture into modern industry, the productive forces evolved under the guidance of the bourgeoisie developed with a rapidity and in a degree unheard of before. But just as the older manufacture, in its time, and handicraft, becoming more developed under its influence, had come into collision with the feudal trammels of the guilds, so now modern industry, in its more complete development, comes into collision with the bounds within which the capitalistic mode of production holds it confined. The new productive forces have already outgrown the capitalistic mode of using them. And this conflict between productive forces and modes of production is not a conflict engendered in the mind of man, like that between original sin and divine justice. It exists, in fact, objectively, outside us, independently of the will and actions even of the men that have brought it on. Modern Socialism is nothing but the reflex, in thought, of this conflict in fact ; its ideal reflection in the minds, first, of the class directly suffering under it, the working-class.

Now, in what does this conflict consist ?

Before capitalistic production, *i.e.,* in the Middle Ages, the system of petty industry obtained generally, based upon the private property of the labourers in their means of production ; in the country, the agriculture of the small peasant, freeman or serf ; in the towns, the handicrafts organised in guilds. The instruments of labour—land, agricultural implements, the workshop, the tool—were the instruments of labour of single individuals, adapted for the use of one worker, and, therefore, of necessity, small, dwarfish, circumscribed. But, for this very reason they belonged, as a rule, to the producer himself. To concentrate these scattered, limited means of production, to enlarge them, to turn them into the powerful levers of production of the present day —this was precisely the historic rôle of capitalist production and of its upholder, the bourgeoisie. In the fourth section of "Capital" Marx has explained in detail, how since the fifteenth century this has been historically worked out through the three phases of simple co-operation, manufacture, and modern industry. But the bourgeoisie, as is also shown there, could not transform these puny means of production into mighty productive forces, without transforming them, at the same time, from means of production of the individual into *social* means of production only workable by a collectivity of men. The spinning-wheel, the handloom, the blacksmith's hammer, were replaced by the spinning-machine, the power-loom, the steam-hammer; the individual workshop, by the factory implying the co-operation of hundreds and thousands of workmen In like manner, production itself changed from a series of individual into a series of social acts, and the products from individual to social products. The yarn, the cloth, the metal articles that now came out of the factory were the joint product of many workers, through whose hands they had successively to pass before they were ready. No one person could say of them : " I made that , this is *my* product."

But where, in a given society, the fundamental form of production is that spontaneous division of labour which creeps in gradually and not upon any preconceived plan, there the pro-

ducts take on the form of *commodities*, whose
mutual exchange, buying and selling, enable the
individual producers to satisfy their manifold
wants. And this was the case in the Middle
Ages. The peasant, *e.g.*, sold to the artisan
agricultural products and bought from him the
products of handicraft. Into this society of individual producers, of commodity-producers, the
new mode of production thrust itself In the
midst of the old division of labour, grown up
spontaneously and upon *no definite plan*, which
had governed the whole of society, now arose
division of labour upon *a definite plan*, as organised in the factory, side by side with *individual*
production appeared *social* production. The
products of both were sold in the same market,
and, therefore, at prices at least approximately
equal. But organisation upon a definite plan
was stronger than spontaneous division of
labour. The factories working with the combined social forces of a collectivity of individuals
produced their commodities far more cheaply
than the individual small producers. Individual
production succumbed in one department after
another. Socialised production revolutionised
all the old methods of production. But its

revolutionary character was, at the same time, so little recognised, that it was, on the contrary, introduced as a means of increasing and developing the production of commodities. When it arose, it found ready-made, and made liberal use of, certain machinery for the production and exchange of commodities; merchants' capital, handicraft, wage-labour. Socialised production thus introducing itself as a new form of the production of commodities, it was a matter of course that under it the old forms of appropriation remained in full swing, and were applied to its products as well.

In the mediæval stage of evolution of the production of commodities, the question as to the owner of the product of labour could not arise. The individual producer, as a rule, had, from raw material belonging to himself, and generally his own handiwork, produced it with his own tools, by the labour of his own hands or of his family. There was no need for him to appropriate the new product. It belonged wholly to him, as a matter of course His property in the product was, therefore, based *upon his own labour*. Even where external help was used, this was, as a rule, of little importance, and

very generally was compensated by something
other than wages. The apprentices and journeymen of the guilds worked less for board and
wages than for education, in order that they
might become master craftsmen themselves.

   Then came the concentration of the means of
production and of the producers in large workshops and manufactories, their transformation
into actual socialised means of production and
socialised producers. But the socialised producers and means of production and their products were still treated, after this change, just
as they had been before, *i.e.,* as the means of
production and the products of individuals.
Hitherto, the owner of the instruments of
labour had himself appropriated the product,
because, as a rule, it was his own product and
the assistance of others was the exception.
Now the owner of the instruments of labour
always appropriated to himself the product,
although it was no longer *his* product but
exclusively the product of the *labour of others.*
Thus, the products now produced socially were
not appropriated by those who had actually set
in motion the means of production and actually
produced the commodities, but by the *capitalists.*

The means of production, and production itself, had become in essence socialised. But they were subjected to a form of appropriation which presupposes the private production of individuals, under which, therefore, every one owns his own product and brings it to market. The mode of production is subjected to this form of appropriation, although it abolishes the conditions upon which the latter rests.[1]

This contradiction, which gives to the new mode of production its capitalistic character, *contains the germ of the whole of the social antagonisms of to-day*. The greater the mastery obtained by the new mode of production over all important fields of production and in all manufacturing countries, the more it reduced individual production to an insignificant residuum, *the more*

[1] It is hardly necessary in this connexion to point out, that, even if the form of appropriation remains the same, the *character* of the appropriation is just as much revolutionised as production is by the changes described above. It is, of course, a very different matter whether I appropriate to myself my own product or that of another. Note in passing that wage-labour, which contains the whole capitalistic mode of production in embryo, is very ancient; in a sporadic, scattered form it existed for centuries alongside of slave-labour. But the embryo could duly develop into the capitalistic mode of production only when the necessary historical pre-conditions had been furnished.

*clearly was brought out the incompatibility of so-
cialised production with capitalistic appropriation.*

The first capitalists found, as we have said,
alongside of other forms of labour, wage-labour
ready-made for them on the market. But it was
exceptional, complementary, accessory, transi-
tory wage-labour. The agricultural labourer,
though, upon occasion, he hired himself out by
the day, had a few acres of his own land on
which he could at all events live at a pinch.
The guilds were so organised that the journeyman of to-day became the master of to-morrow.
But all this changed, as soon as the means of
production became socialised and concentrated
in the hands of capitalists. The means of production, as well as the product, of the individual
producer became more and more worthless ;
there was nothing left for him but to turn wage-
worker under the capitalist. Wage-labour,
aforetime the exception and accessory, now became the rule and basis of all production; aforetime complementary, it now became the sole
remaining function of the worker. The wage-
worker for a time became a wage-worker for
life. The number of these permanent wage-
workers was further enormously increased by

the breaking-up of the feudal system that occurred at the same time, by the disbanding of
the retainers of the feudal lords, the eviction of
the peasants from their homesteads, etc. The
separation was made complete between the
means of production concentrated in the hands
of the capitalists on the one side, and the
producers, possessing nothing but their labour-
power, on the other. *The contradiction between
socialised production and capitalistic appropriation manifested itself as the antagonism of
proletariat and bourgeoisie.*

We have seen that the capitalistic mode of
production thrust its way into a society of
commodity-producers, of individual producers,
whose social bond was the exchange of their
products. But every society, based upon the
production of commodities, has this peculiarity:
that the producers have lost control over their
own social inter-relations. Each man produces
for himself with such means of production as
he may happen to have, and for such exchange
as he may require to satisfy his remaining wants.
No one knows how much of his particular article
is coming on the market, nor how much of it will
be wanted. No one knows whether his indi-

vidual product will meet an actual demand, whether he will be able to make good his cost of production or even to sell his commodity at all. Anarchy reigns in socialised production.

But the production of commodities, like every other form of production, has its peculiar, inherent laws inseparable from it; and these laws work, despite anarchy, in and through anarchy. They reveal themselves in the only persistent form of social inter-relations, *i.e.*, in exchange, and here they affect the individual producers as compulsory laws of competition. They are, at first, unknown to these producers themselves, and have to be discovered by them gradually and as the result of experience. They work themselves out, therefore, independently of the producers, and in antagonism to them, as inexorable natural laws of their particular form of production. The product governs the producers.

In mediæval society, especially in the earlier centuries, production was essentially directed towards satisfying the wants of the individual. It satisfied, in the main, only the wants of the producer and his family. Where relations of personal dependence existed, as in the country it also helped to satisfy the wants of the feudal lord. In all this there was, therefore, no exchange; the products, consequently, did not assume the character of commodities. The family of the peasant produced almost everything they wanted: clothes and furniture, as well as means of subsistence. Only when it began to produce more than was sufficient to supply its own wants and the payments in kind to the feudal lord, only then did it also produce commodities. This surplus, thrown into socialised exchange and offered for sale, became commodities.

The artisans of the towns, it is true, had from the first to produce for exchange. But they, also, themselves supplied the greatest part of their own individual wants. They had gardens and plots of land. They turned their cattle out into the communal forest, which, also, yielded them timber and firing. The women spun flax, wool, and so forth. Production for the purpose of exchange, production of commodities, was only in its infancy. Hence, exchange was restricted, the market narrow, the methods of production stable; there was local exclusiveness without, local unity within; the mark [1] in the country, in the town, the guild.

[1] *See Appendix.*

But with the extension of the production of commodities, and especially with the introduction of the capitalist mode of production, the laws of commodity-production, hitherto latent, came into action more openly and with greater force. The old bonds were loosened, the old exclusive limits broken through, the producers were more and more turned into independent, isolated producers of commodities. It became apparent that the production of society at large was ruled by absence of plan, by accident, by anarchy ; and this anarchy grew to greater and greater height. But the chief means by aid of which the capitalist mode of production intensified this anarchy of socialised production, was the exact opposite of anarchy. It was the increasing organisation of production, upon a social basis, in every individual productive establishment. By this, the old, peaceful, stable condition of things was ended. Wherever this organisation of production was introduced into a branch of industry. it brooked no other method of production by its side The field of labour became a battle-ground. The great geographical discoveries, and the colonisation following upon them, multiplied markets and quickened the transformation of handicraft into manufacture. The war did not simply break out between the individual producers of particular localities. The local struggles begat in their turn national conflicts, the commercial wars of the seventeenth and the eighteenth centuries.

Finally, modern industry and the opening of the world-market made the struggle universal, and at the same time gave it an unheard-of virulence. Advantages in natural or artificial conditions of production now decide the existence or non-existence of individual capitalists, as well as of whole industries and countries. He that falls is remorselessly cast aside   It is the Darwinian struggle of the individual for existence transferred from Nature to society with intensified violence. The conditions of existence natural to the animal appear as the final term of human development. The contradiction between socialised production and capitalistic appropriation now presents itself as *an antagonism between the organisation of production in the individual workshop and the anarchy of production in society generally.*

The capitalistic mode of production moves in these two forms of the antagonism immanen*

to it from its very origin. It is never able to
get out of that "vicious circle," which Fourier
had already discovered. What Fourier could
not, indeed, see in his time is, that this circle is
gradually narrowing; that the movement becomes more and more a spiral, and must come
to an end, like the movement of the planets,
by collision with the centre. It is the compelling force of anarchy in the production of
society at large that more and more completely
turns the great majority of men into proletarians;
and it is the masses of the proletariat again who
will finally put an end to anarchy in production.
It is the compelling force of anarchy in social
production that turns the limitless perfectibility
of machinery under modern industry into a compulsory law by which every individual industrial
capitalist must perfect his machinery more and
more, under penalty of ruin.

But the perfecting of machinery is the making human labour superfluous. If the introduction and increase of machinery means the
displacement of millions of manual, by a few
machine, workers, improvement in machinery
means the displacement of more and more of
the machine-workers themselves. It means, in

the last instance, the production of a number of available wage-workers in excess of the average needs of capital, the formation of a complete industrial reserve army, as I called it in 1845,[1] available at the times when industry is working at high pressure, to be cast out upon the street when the inevitable crash comes, a constant dead weight upon the limbs of the working-class in its struggle for existence with capital, a regulator for the keeping of wages down to the low level that suits the interests of capital. Thus it comes about, to quote Marx, that machinery becomes the most powerful weapon in the war of capital against the working-class ; that the instruments of labour constantly tear the means of subsistence out of the hands of the labourer ; that the very product of the worker is turned into an instrument for his subjugation. Thus it comes about that the economising of the instruments of labour becomes at the same time, from the outset, the most reckless waste of labour-power, and robbery based upon the normal conditions under which labour functions ; that machinery,

[1] "The Condition of the Working-Class in England" (Sonnenschein & Co.), p. 84.

"the most powerful instrument for shortening
labour-time, becomes the most unfailing means
for placing every moment of the labourer's time
and that of his family at the disposal of the capitalist for the purpose of expanding the value of
his capital" ("Capital," English edition, p. 406).
Thus it comes about that over-work of some becomes the preliminary condition for the idleness
of others, and that modern industry, which
hunts after new consumers over the whole
world, forces the consumption of the masses at
home down to a starvation minimum, and in
doing thus destroys its own home market.
"The law that always equilibrates the relative surplus population, or industrial reserve
army, to the extent and energy of accumulation,
this law rivets the labourer to capital more
firmly than the wedges of Vulcan did Prome-
theus to the rock. It establishes an accumulation of misery, corresponding with accumulation
of capital. Accumulation of wealth at one pole
is, therefore, at the same time, accumulation of
misery, agony of toil, slavery, ignorance,
brutality, mental degradation, at the opposite
pole, *i.e.*, on the side of the class that produces
its own product in the form of capital." (Marx'

" Capital " [Sonnenschein & Co.], p. 661.)
And to expect any other division of the
products from the capitalistic mode of production is the same as expecting the electrodes
of a battery not to decompose acidulated water,
not to liberate oxygen at the positive, hydrogen
at the negative pole, so long as they are connected with the battery.

We have seen that the ever-increasing
perfectibility of modern machinery is, by the
anarchy of social production, turned into a
compulsory law that forces the individual
industrial capitalist always to improve his
machinery, always to increase its productive force. The bare possibility of extend-
ing the field of production is transformed
for him into a similar compulsory law. The
enormous expansive force of modern industry, compared with which that of gases is
mere child's play, appears to us now as a
necessity for expansion, both qualitative and
quantitative, that laughs at all resistance. Such
resistance is offered by consumption, by sales,
by the markets for the products of modern
industry. But the capacity for extension, ex-
tensive and intensive, of the markets is prim-

arily governed by quite different laws, that
work much less energetically. The extension
of the markets cannot keep pace with the
extension of production. The collision becomes inevitable, and as this cannot produce
any real solution so long as it does not break
in pieces the capitalist mode of production,
the collisions become periodic. Capitalist
production has begotten another " vicious
circle."

As a matter of fact, since 1825, when the
first general crisis broke out, the whole industrial and commercial world, production and
exchange among all civilised peoples and their
more or less barbaric hangers-on, are thrown
out of joint about once every ten years. Commerce is at a standstill, the markets are glutted,
products accumulate, as multitudinous as they
are unsaleable, hard cash disappears, credit
vanishes, factories are closed, the mass of the
workers are in want of the means of subsistence, because they have produced too much of
the means of subsistence; bankruptcy follows
upon bankruptcy, execution upon execution.
The stagnation lasts for years; productive
forces and products are wasted and destroyed

wholesale, until the accumulated mass of commodities finally filter off, more or less depreciated in value, until production and exchange gradually begin to move again. Little by little the pace quickens. It becomes a trot The industrial trot breaks into a canter, the canter in turn grows into the headlong gallop of a perfect steeplechase of industry, commercial credit, and speculation, which finally, after breakneck leaps, ends where it began—in the ditch of a crisis. And so over and over again. We have now, since the year 1825, gone through this five times, and at the present moment (1877) we are going through it for the sixth time And the character of these crises is so clearly defined that Fourier hit all of them off, when he described the first as *crise pléthorique*," a crisis from plethora.

In these crises, the contradiction between socialised production and capitalist appropriation ends in a violent explosion. The circulation of commodities is, for the time being, stopped. Money, the means of circulation, becomes a hindrance to circulation. All the laws of production and circulation of commodities are turned upside down. The economic collision has reached its apogee. *The mode of pro-*

duction is in rebellion against the mode of exchange.

The fact that the socialised organisation of production within the factory has developed so far that it has become incompatible with the anarchy of production in society, which exists side by side with and dominates it, is brought home to the capitalists themselves by the violent concentration of capital that occurs during crises, through the ruin of many large, and a still greater number of small, capitalists. The whole mechanism of the capitalist mode of production breaks down under the pressure of the productive forces, its own creations . It is no longer able to turn all this mass of means of production into capital. They lie fallow, and for that very reason the industrial reserve army must also lie fallow   Means of production, means of subsistence, available labourers, all the elements of production and of general wealth, are present in abundance   But "abundance becomes the source of distress and want" (Fourier) because it is the very thing that prevents the transformation of the means of production and subsistence into capital: For in capitalistic society the means of production can only function when they have undergone a preliminary transformation into capital, into the means of exploiting human labour-power. The necessity of this transformation into capital of the means of production and subsistence stands like a ghost between these and the workers. It alone prevents the coming together of the material and personal levers of production; it alone forbids the means of production to function, the workers to work and live. On the one hand, therefore, the capitalistic mode of production stands convicted of its own incapacity to further direct these productive forces. On the other, these productive forces themselves, with increasing energy, press forward to the removal of the existing contradiction, to the abolition of their quality as capital, to the *practical recognition of their character as social productive forces.*

This rebellion of the productive forces, as they grow more and more powerful, against their quality as capital, this stronger and stronger command that their social character shall be recognised, forces the capitalist class itself to treat them more and more as social productive forces. so far as this is possible under capitalist

conditions. The period of industrial high pressure, with its unbounded inflation of credit, not
less than the crash itself, by the collapse of great
capitalist establishments, tends to bring about
that form of the socialisation of great masses of
means of production, which we meet with in the
different kinds of joint-stock companies. Many
of these means of production and of distribution
are, from the outset, so colossal, that, like the
railroads, they exclude all other forms of
capitalistic exploitation. At a further stage of
evolution this form also becomes insufficient.
The producers on a large scale in a particular
branch of industry in a particular country unite
in a "Trust," a union for the purpose of regu-
lating production. They determine the total
amount to be produced, parcel it out among
themselves, and thus enforce the selling price
fixed beforehand. But trusts of this kind, as
soon as business becomes bad, are generally liable
to break up, and, on this very account, compel a
yet greater concentration of association. The
whole of the particular industry is turned into
one gigantic joint-stock company; internal
competition gives place to the internal monopoly
of this one company. This has happened in

1890 with the English *alkali* production, which is now, after the fusion of 48 large works, in the hands of one company, conducted upon a single plan, and with a capital of £6,000,000.

In the trusts, freedom of competition changes into its very opposite—into monopoly; and the production without any definite plan of capitalistic society capitulates to the production upon a definite plan of the invading socialistic society. Certainly this is so far still to the benefit and advantage of the capitalists. But in this case the exploitation is so palpable that it must break down. No nation will put up with production conducted by trusts, with so barefaced an exploitation of the community by a small band of dividend-mongers.

In any case, with trusts or without, the official representative of capitalist society—the State—will ultimately have to undertake the direction of production.[1] This necessity for conversion into

[1] I say "have to." For only when the means of production and distribution have *actually* outgrown the form of management by joint-stock companies, and when, therefore, the taking them over by the State has become *economically* inevitable, only then—even if it is the State of to-day that effects this—is there an economic advance, the attainment of another step preliminary to the taking over of all productive forces by society itself.

State-property is felt first in the great institutions for intercourse and communication—the post-office, the telegraphs, the railways.

If the crises demonstrate the incapacity of the bourgeoisie for managing any longer modern productive forces, the transformation of the great establishments for production and distribution into joint-stock companies, trusts, and State property, show how unnecessary the

But of late, since Bismarck went in for State-ownership of industrial establishments, a kind of spurious Socialism has arisen, degenerating, now and again, into something of flunkeyism, that without more ado declares *all* State-ownership, even of the Bismarckian sort, to be socialistic. Certainly, if the taking over by the State of the tobacco industry is socialistic, then Napoleon and Metternich must be numbered among the founders of Socialism. If the Belgian State, for quite ordinary political and financial reasons, itself constructed its chief railway lines ; if Bismarck, not under any economic compulsion, took over for the State the chief Prussian lines, simply to be the better able to have them in hand in case of war, to bring up the railway employees as voting cattle for the Government, and especially to create for himself a new source of income independent of parliamentary votes—this was, in no sense, a socialistic measure, directly or indirectly, consciously or unconsciously. Otherwise, the Royal Maritime Company, the Royal porcelain manufacture, and even the regimental tailor of the army would also be socialistic institutions, or even, as was seriously proposed by a sly dog in Frederick William III.'s reign, the taking over by the State of the brothels.

bourgeoisie are for that purpose. All the
social functions of the capitalist are now performed by salaried employees. The capitalist
has no further social function than that of
pocketing dividends, tearing off coupons, and
gambling on the Stock Exchange, where the
different capitalists despoil one another of their
capital. At first the capitalistic mode of production forces out the workers. Now it forces
out the capitalists, and reduces them, just as it
reduced the workers, to the ranks of the surplus population, although not immediately into
those of the industrial reserve army.

But the transformation, either into joint-
stock companies and trusts, or into State-
ownership, does not do away with the capitalistic nature of the productive forces. In the
joint-stock companies and trusts this is obvious.
And the modern State, again, is only the
organisation that bourgeois society takes on
in order to support the external conditions of
the capitalist mode of production against the en-
croachments, as well of the workers as of individual capitalists. The modern State, no matter
what its form, is essentially a capitalist machine,
the state of the capitalists, the ideal personifica-

tion of the total national capital. The more it
proceeds to the taking over of productive forces,.
the more does it actually become the national
capitalist, the more citizens does it exploit. The
workers remain wage-workers—proletarians.
The capitalist relation is not done away with.
It is rather brought to a head. But, brought to
a head, it topples over. State-ownership of the
productive forces is not the solution of the conflict, but concealed within it are the technical
conditions that form the elements of that solution.

This solution can only consist in the practical
recognition of the social nature of the modern
forces of production, and therefore in the
harmonising the modes of production, appropriation, and exchange with the socialised
character of the means of production. And
this can only come about by society openly
and directly taking possession of the productive forces which have outgrown all control
except that of society as a whole. The
social character of the means of production
and of the products to-day reacts against the
producers, periodically disrupts all production and exchange, acts only like a law of
Nature working blindly, forcibly, destructively.

But with the taking over by society of the productive forces, the social character of the means of production and of the products will be utilised by the producers with a perfect understanding of its nature, and instead of being a source of disturbance and periodical collapse, will become the most powerful lever of production itself.

Active social forces work exactly like natural forces : blindly, forcibly, destructively, so long as we do not understand, and reckon with, them. But when once we understand them, when once we grasp their action, their direction, their effects, it depends only upon ourselves to subject them more and more to our own will, and by means of them to reach our own ends. And this holds quite especially of the mighty productive forces of to-day. As long as we obstinately refuse to understand the nature and the character of these social means of action—and this understanding goes against the grain of the capitalist mode of production and its defenders—so long these forces are at work in spite of us, in opposition to us, so long they master us, as we have shown above in detail.

But when once their nature is understood, they can, in the hands of the producers working together, be transformed from master demons into willing servants. The difference is as that between the destructive force of electricity in the lightning of the storm, and electricity under command in the telegraph and the voltaic arc; the difference between a conflagration, and fire working in the service of man. With this recognition at last of the real nature of the productive forces of to-day, the social anarchy of production gives place to a social regulation of production upon a definite plan, according to the needs of the community and of each individual. Then the capitalist mode of appropriation, in which the product enslaves first the producer and then the appropriator, is replaced by the mode of appropriation of the products that is based upon the nature of the modern means of production; upon the one hand, direct social appropriation, as means to the maintenance and extension of production—on the other, direct individual appropriation, as means of subsistence and of enjoyment.

Whilst the capitalist mode of production

more and more completely transforms the
great majority of the population into proletarians, it creates the power which, under
penalty of its own destruction, is forced to
accomplish this revolution. Whilst it forces
on more and more the transformation of the
vast means of production, already socialised,
into State property, it shows itself the way
to accomplishing this revolution. *The pro-*
letariat seizes political power and turns the
means of production into State property.

But, in doing this, it abolishes itself as
proletariat, abolishes all class distinctions and
class antagonisms, abolishes also the State
as State. Society thus far, based upon class
antagonisms, had need of the State. That is,
of an organisation of the particular class which
was *pro tempore* the exploiting class, an organisation for the purpose of preventing any interference from without with the existing conditions
of production, and therefore, especially, for the
purpose of forcibly keeping the exploited classes
in the condition of oppression corresponding
with the given mode of production (slavery,
serfdom, wage-labour). The State was the
official representative of society as a whole;

the gathering of it together into a visible
embodiment. But it was this only in so far
as it was the State of that class which itself
represented, for the time being, society as a
whole; in ancient times, the State of slave-
owning citizens; in the middle ages, the feudal
lords; in our own time, the bourgeoisie.
When at last it becomes the real representative
of the whole of society, it renders itself unnecessary. As soon as there is no longer
any social class to be held in subjection; as
soon as class rule, and the individual struggle
for existence based upon our present anarchy
in production, with the collisions and excesses
arising from these, are removed, nothing more
remains to be repressed, and a special repres-
sive force, a State, is no longer necessary.
The first act by virtue of which the State
really constitutes itself the representative of
the whole of society—the taking possession of
the means of production in the name of
society—this is, at the same time, its last
independent act as a State. State interference
in social relations becomes, in one domain
after another, superfluous, and then dies out
of itself; the government of persons is replaced

by the administration of things, and by the conduct of processes of production. The State is not " abolished." *It dies out.* This gives the measure of the value of the phrase " a free 'State," both as to its justifiable use at times, by agitators, and as to its ultimate scientific insufficiency, and also of the demands of the so-called anarchists for the abolition of the State out of hand.

Since the historical appearance of the capitalist mode of production, the appropriation by society of all the means of production has often been dreamed of, more or less vaguely, by individuals, as well as by sects, as the ideal of the future. But it could become possible, could become a historical necessity, only when the actual conditions for its realisation were there. Like every other social advance, it becomes practicable, not by men understanding that the existence of classes is in contradiction to justice, equality, etc., not by the mere willingness to abolish these classes, but by virtue of certain new economic conditions. The Separation of society into an exploiting and an exploited class, a ruling and an oppressed class, was the necessary consequence of the deficient and restricted development of production in former times. So long as the total social labour only yields a produce which but slightly exceeds that barely necessary for the existence of all; so long, therefore, as labour engages all or almost all the time of the great majority of the members of society—so long, of necessity, this society is divided into classes. Side by side with the great majority, exclusively bond slaves to labour, arises a class freed from directly productive labour, which looks after the general affairs of society; the direction of labour, State business, law, science, art, etc. It is, therefore, the law of division of labour that lies at the basis of the division into classes. But this does not prevent this division into classes from being carried out by means of violence and robbery, trickery and fraud. It does not prevent the ruling class, once having the upper hand, from consolidating its power at the expense of the working-class, from turning their social leadership into an intensified exploitation of the masses.

But if, upon this showing, division into classes has a certain historical justification, it has this only for a given period, only under

given social conditions. It was based upon
the insufficiency of production. It will be
swept away by the complete development
of modern productive forces. And, in fact,
the abolition of classes in society presupposes
a degree of historical evolution, at which the
existence, not simply of this or that particular
ruling class, but of any ruling class at all, and,
therefore, the existence of class distinction itself
has become an obsolete anachronism It presupposes, therefore, the development of production carried out to a degree at which
appropriation of the means of production and
of the products, and, with this, of political
domination, of the monopoly of culture, and of
intellectual leadership by a particular class of
society, has become not only superfluous, but
economically, politically, intellectually a hindrance to development.

This point is now reached. Their political
and intellectual bankruptcy is scarcely any longer
a secret to the bourgeoisie themselves. Their
economic bankruptcy recurs regularly every
ten years. In every crisis, society is suffocated
beneath the weight of its own productive forces
and products, which it cannot use, and stands

helpless, face to face with the absurd contradiction that the producers have nothing to
consume, because consumers are wanting.
The expansive force of the means of production bursts the bonds that the capitalist mode
of production had imposed upon them. Their
deliverance from these bonds is the one pre-
condition for an unbroken, constantly-acceler-
ated development of the productive forces, and
therewith for a practically unlimited increase of
production itself. Nor is this all. The socialised appropriation of the means of production
does away, not only with the present artificial
restrictions upon production, but also with the
positive waste and devastation of productive
forces and products that are at the present
time the inevitable concomitants of production,
and that reach their height in the crises.
Further, it sets free for the community at large
a mass of means of production and of products,
by doing away with the senseless extravagance
of the ruling classes of to-day; and their political representatives. The possibility of securing
for every member of society, by means of
socialised production, an existence not only
fully sufficient materially, and becoming day

by day more full, but an existence guaranteeing to all the free development and exercise of their physical and mental faculties—this possibility is now for the first time here, but *it is here.*[1]

With the seizing of the means of production by society, production of commodities is done away with, and, simultaneously, the mastery of the product over the producer. Anarchy in social production is replaced by systematic, definite organisation. The struggle for individual existence disappears. Then for the first time, man, in a certain sense, is finally marked off from the rest of the animal kingdom, and emerges from mere animal conditions of exist-

[1]. A few figures may serve to give an approximate idea of the enormous expansive force of the modern means of production, even under capitalist pressure. According to Mr. Giffen, the total wealth of Great Britain and Ireland amounted, in round numbers, in

1814 to £2,200,000,000.
1865 to £6,100,000,000.
1875 to £8,500,000,000.

As an instance of the squandering of means of production and of products during a crisis, the total loss in the German iron industry alone, in the crisis 1873-78, was given at the second German Industrial Congress (Berlin, February 21, 1878) as £22,750,000.

ence into really human ones. The whole sphere
of the conditions of life which environ man, and
which have hitherto ruled man, now comes
under the dominion and control of man, who
for the first time becomes the real, conscious
lord of Nature, because he has now become
master of his own social organisation. The
laws of his own social action, hitherto standing face to face with man as laws of Nature
foreign to, and dominating, him, will then be
used with full understanding, and so mastered
by him. Man's own social organisation,
hitherto confronting him as a necessity imposed by Nature and history, now becomes
the result of his own free action. The ex-
traneous objective forces that have hitherto
governed history, pass under the control of
man himself. Only from that time will man
himself more and more consciously, make his
own history—only from that time will the social
causes set in movement by him have, in the
main and in a constantly growing measure, the
results intended by him. It is the ascent of
man from the kingdom of necessity to the kingdom of freedom.

Let us briefly sum up our sketch of historical evolution.

1. *Mediæval Society.*—Individual production on a small scale. Means of production adapted for individual use, hence primitive, ungainly, petty, dwarfed in action. Production for immediate consumption, either of the producer himself or of his feudal lord. Only where an excess of production over this consumption occurs is such excess offered for sale, enters into exchange. Production of commodities, therefore, only in its infancy. But already it contains within itself, in embryo, *anarchy in the production of society at large*

II. *Capitalist Revolution.* — Transformation of industry, at first by means of simple co-operation and manufacture. Concentration of the means of production, hitherto scattered, into great workshops. As a consequence, their transformation from individual to social means of production—a transformation which does not, on the whole, affect the form of exchange. The old forms of appropriation remain in force. The capitalist appears. In his capacity as owner

of the means of production, he also appro-
priates the products and turns them into commodities. Production has become a *social* act.
Exchange and appropriation continue to be
individual acts, the acts of individuals. *The*
social product is appropriated by the individual
capitalist. Fundamental contradiction, whence
arise all the contradictions in which our present
day society moves, and which modern industry
brings to light.

A. Severance of the producer from the means
of production. Condemnation of the worker
to wage-labour for life. *Antagonism between*
the proletariat and the bourgeoisie.

B. Growing predominance and increasing
effectiveness of the laws governing the production of commodities. Unbridled competition.
Contradiction between socialised organisation in
the individual factory and social anarchy in
production as a whole.

C. On the one hand, perfecting of machinery,
made by competition compulsory for each individual manufacturer, and complemented by a

constantly growing displacement of labourers. *Industrial reserve-army,* On the other hand, unlimited extension of production, also compulsory under competition, for every manufacturer. On both sides, unheard of development of productive forces, excess of supply over demand, over-production, glutting of the markets, crises every ten years, the vicious circle excess here, of means of production and products—excess there, of labourers, without employment and without means of existence But these two levers of production and of social well-being are unable to work together, because the capitalist form of production prevents the productive forces from working and the products from circulating, unless they are first turned into capital—which their very superabundance prevents The contradiction has grown into an absurdity *The mode of production rises in rebellion against the form of exchange.* The bourgeoisie are convicted of incapacity further to manage their own social productive forces.

D Partial recognition of the social character of the productive forces forced upon the capitalists themselves. Taking over of the great institutions for production and communication, first by joint-stock companies, later on by trusts, then by the State. The bourgeoisie demonstrated to be a superfluous class. All its social functions are now performed by salaried employees.

III. *Proletarian Revolution.*—Solution of the contradictions. The proletariat seizes the public power, and by means of this transforms the socialised means of production, slipping from the hands of the bourgeoisie, into public property. By this act, the proletariat frees the means of production from the character of capital they have thus far borne, and gives their socialised character complete freedom to work itself out. Socialised production upon a predetermined plan becomes henceforth possible. The development of production makes the existence of different classes of society thenceforth an anachronism. In proportion as anarchy in social production vanishes, the political authority of the State dies out. Man, at last the master of his own form of social organisation, becomes at the same time the lord over Nature, his own master—free.

To accomplish this act of universal emancipation is the <u>historical mission</u> of the modern proletariat. To thoroughly comprehend the historical conditions and thus the very nature of this act, to impart to the now oppressed proletarian class a full knowledge of the conditions and of the meaning of the momentous act it is called upon to accomplish, this is the task of the theoretical expression of the proletarian movement, scientific Socialism.

CPSIA information can be obtained
at www.ICGtesting.com
Printed in the USA
BVOW03*2151100817
491795BV00003B/10/P